Catherine Owen

Progressive Housekeeping - keeping house without knowing how

Catherine Owen

Progressive Housekeeping - keeping house without knowing how

ISBN/EAN: 9783744736855

Printed in Europe, USA, Canada, Australia, Japan

Cover: Foto ©Suzi / pixelio.de

More available books at **www.hansebooks.com**

PROGRESSIVE HOUSEKEEPING

KEEPING HOUSE WITHOUT KNOWING HOW, AND KNOWING HOW TO KEEP HOUSE WELL

BY

CATHERINE OWEN

AUTHOR OF "TEN DOLLARS ENOUGH," "MOLLY BISHOP'S FAMILY,"
"GENTLE BREADWINNERS," ETC.

BOSTON AND NEW YORK
HOUGHTON, MIFFLIN AND COMPANY
The Riverside Press, Cambridge
1889

CONTENTS.

———◆———

CHAPTER I.

CHAPTER II.

CHAPTER III.

CHAPTER IV.

CHAPTER V.

CHAPTER VI.

CHAPTER VII.

CHAPTER VIII.

PROGRESSIVE HOUSEKEEPING.

CHAPTER I.

A FEW INTRODUCTORY REMARKS.

A SERIES of papers on housekeeping is a very easy thing to project, but very difficult to make really useful to the general public. At first sight it seemed, with so many "Housekeepers' Assistants," "Domestic Cyclopædias," and household guides whose existence came to one's memory at once, that the last word on the subject must have been said, and the demand for more was only to be accounted for by the fact that the many books with housekeeping titles were too cumbrous in form, and, instead of the many, one book was needed, containing the gist of all, supplemented and illuminated where obscure, by actual and varied experience of author or compiler, who would assist the different classes of housekeepers to adapt the instructions to their own needs.

With this idea in view the writer prepared for weeks of diligent reading and digestion of innumerable books on the subject, and not without some dread of the work. A first raid was made on the library catalogues under the subject, "Domestic Economy," and book after book, with the most promising titles, opened. But the "Complete guide to every department of Housekeeping, from Poultry Yard to the Boudoir," instead of being specially devoted to *Housekeeping*, was found to be a very valuable book containing recipes for everything, from engraving on glass to making artificial flowers, a very useful book, but rather more useful to a carpenter or a druggist than to the housekeeper. "Housekeeper's Assistants," "Housekeeping Made Easy," "Complete Housekeepers," all were found to be *cooking* books, more or less good, but *cooking* books pure and simple. This was rather a surprising result, and further search revealed the fact that in the largest library in New York, not one book was to be found treating specially of housekeeping. Housekeeping titles were frequent enough, from "Housekeeper's Complete Assistant" of 1796 to the present day, but cooking books all,—nay, I do the latter-day cooking books wrong, for I found more useful housekeeping information in the few prefatory pages of several latter-day books on cooking, and called simply "Cook Books," notably Mrs. Helen Campbell's "The Easiest way," than in all the mass of Housekeepers' Manuals I could find. After the libraries, booksellers' catalogues were consulted, but the result of considerable search seems to have but one conclusion,—*a book on housekeeping* has yet to be written ; it cannot be a compiled work, for there is nothing to compile from. It is, therefore, with a very keen appreciation of the difficulty of the task before me that I commence a series of papers which, however they may fall short of the universal usefulness hoped for, will be written with earnest effort to approach that point. Of course, not every one will be suited. Old and successful housekeepers, who have made rigid and undeviating order their rule through life and see the results in domestic machinery that goes like clock work, will disapprove of the elastic conditions I would advocate, while to the latitudinarian housemother (and I have known very happy families brought up with a joyous disregard of all hours or rules, but—and the but is very large—the means were ample) limited means and disregard of order mean the most sordid discomfort.

My sermon, however, will always be from the same text : "Keep house, in order to live comfortably ; don't live in order to keep house." The ideal housekeeper is the one who, without seeming to give much heed to the wheels of her household machinery, has it in such perfect running order that it seems to go of itself. Of such a one we shall hear it said, "she has such good fortune with her servants," etc. Once suited, she probably keeps them for years, and her friends ignore the weeks or months of search that may have preceded this happy state. Such women are rare ; they have the administrative gift,—the knack of getting things done for them in the way they wish, and knowing quite well the way things should be done. We can each recall, perhaps, one such easy-going house, where everything seems to fall into its place, where there appear to be no immutable laws, and yet we may be sure the price of this seeming ease and smoothness is constant vigilance and patience on the part of the house mistress.

Far more familiar to us is the strenuous housekeeper, whose days—and who may say how much of her nights—are pervaded by anxiety as to her servants and children, who is only miserably conscious that, try as she will, she cannot realize her own ideal of housekeeping. She allows herself no leisure or respite, but only by such effort does it seem possible to have the meals served punctually, and with the neatness she loves. If her eye and hand are withdrawn chaos reigns.

The difference between these two women is only to be accounted for by temperament, to be recognized and regretted, but not argued with. Greatly as the friends of the woman whose nervous energy does not allow her to delegate her work successfully to others, may deplore her waste of strength and life, no amount of argument can change her nature.

There is yet another kind of housekeeper, which I may briefly describe as the martinet. Such a one will need no information that these papers can impart; she would scarcely consider that the easy sway of my ideal housekeeper, whose elastic order is seen in its results, but never heard of, is housekeeping at all. The great thing to be desired in housekeeping, is the *comfort* of all who live in the house. This goes before every other thing; to ensure it, order, punctuality, and cleanliness are necessary, but if the order or cleanliness are obtrusive, comfort is impossible.

I take for granted that those who will be most interested in these articles are women who find house-keeping a severe and thankless task, which they, perhaps, have entered upon without preparation or experience, and believe that with more knowledge their task will be easier ; or the young woman just going to keep house, who is determined to fit herself for the task.

I am not hoping in these papers to say the last word on housekeeping. There will be oversights, and some short comings, possibly, that are not oversights, but caused by the exigencies of time and space. Nothing less than a book the size of Webster's Un-abridged could contain all the details of housekeep-ing. My hope is to tell in the Daily Programme, not only the order of work, but how that work is to be done ; how the best results are to be obtained with least labor, which is or should be, the essence of *progress in housekeeping.* Mrs. Gamp says *"there's hart in sticking in a pin,"* and, although many may not know it, there's art in scrubbing a floor or table so that the labor expended may tell. Windows may be better cleaned in five minutes the right way, than in ten the wrong way, and so on through all the work ; the right way is the easiest way, and there is always a right way, although many may think that it comes naturally. I do not know of any book that gives methods of work ; it may be that my effort to do so will not be a success, but at least the effort will be an earnest one.

The plan I have adopted to avoid repetition, as one day's work before breakfast is the same as another, is to begin by giving the early morning work for one day, as a rule, varied by circumstances, for all other days, and so with all other work. I take up the work one day where it left off the day before. What I call the " extra " work of the day, is the work that does not go on every day, as the fire lighting, cooking, and dish washing do. The " extra " work of washing, ironing, thorough sweeping, weekly scrubbing and polishing, I shall give day by day, with directions for doing them and such recipes as pertain to the subject, until all that I can explain is explained ; more particularly shall I try to supply any missing links there may be between books already published and the reader. I am aware that I shall tell some well known facts, and that many of my readers will say, " surely, every school girl knows how to make a fire ;" yet it is astonishing how many young married women there are, who do not know very simple things. How should they know, so many of them just leave boarding school to pass a few gay months and then marry ? One of these may say with equal impatience, " But how am I to make a fire ? Mine never burns." I want to leave no margin for what any one knows or ought to know, and I hope the more experienced will pardon what is to them a thrice told tale.

No one can lay down rules that will fit every case ; the utmost that can be done is to prescribe a course that would seem to meet the needs of the majority. The order of work may differ where a woman has to be her own cook and house maid, as well as mother and wife ; she, less fortunate than the maid, who finds the whole work of a house so hard, cannot pursue the "even tenor of her way," going uninterruptedly from task to task, but is subject to every kind of interruption. She, therefore, that she may be able to be mother and wife and hostess, may find it well to reverse the usual order of work, and instead, we'll say of washing the breakfast dishes and putting them away and seeing the kitchen in order before leaving it, she may find it necessary to leave that till the sitting-room is dusted and the front of the house and bed-rooms arranged, because while she washes the dishes she can watch the bread or cake baking, or the dinner.

Every woman who has no assistance in her work should so arrange it, that it will be easiest for herself, and give thought to this end, and not to do things because " my mother, or Mrs. So and so," did them that way. In this rapid country of ours, things change every day, and there are a hundred labor-saving arrangements, to-day, for one that our mothers had. Avail yourself of every one, even if it only gives you more time to rest. Don't stand rubbing vegetables or fruit through a colander when there is a machine that will do it better in a quarter of the time. Twenty dollars (less than two months wages) spent in labor-saving articles, will be worth a hundred in health and strength. I do not mean, of course, that you are to encumber your kitchen with all the impossible patent articles that appear for a season and then go to swell the limbo of useless inventions, but when a two dollar chopping machine will chop hash, or steak, or sausage in five minutes better than you can in twenty, it is worth while to get it.   The sweeping machine is a most useful article, not for thorough sweeping, but for the daily brushing up necessary in dining and sitting-room.

Of these, and such as these, avail yourself to the extent of your power.   I can address myself directly only to one type of household in these papers.   I take the one most frequently met with in this country,—the small family of four or five, with one servant or none, although, indirectly, I shall try to give some useful information to other classes, even to that class who, since they keep house for others, should need it least—boarding-house keepers.

CHAPTER II.

IT is generally assumed that housekeeping comes naturally to women, that the girl who has been all her life so busy acquiring (or imparting) education and accomplishments that she has had no chance of learning her mother's ways—will, when she finds herself in her own house, know exactly what to do as by inspiration. Who will ever know the bewildered efforts, the failures, the tears, and we will hope, the laughter, that have ushered in the experience of many young wives. But as we must take things as they are, not as they ought to be, and young women will still marry and trust to inspiration, I will say the next best thing to having had actual experience, is to have a theory of housekeeping. Read all you can find on that subject and kindred subjects, and think the matter out, that is to say form some plan, not too ambitious, and then try to carry it out as nearly as comfort will permit.

Your plan perhaps may be something such as I shall indicate in these papers, but it may happen, that you will not find it quite suit your circumstances ; then adapt it. Do not of all things have any cast iron rules, which *must* be carried out. Let even the sacred washing day go by, if it interferes with your own or your family's comfort. At the same time the regular order of work should not be lightly or capriciously changed, unless you would have your house always in disorder, your time consumed, and your family uncomfortable.

A very good order of work is :

Monday, washing.
Tuesday, ironing.
Wednesday, mending.
Thursday, cleaning silver, preserving, etc.
Friday, sweeping, and window cleaning.
Saturday, thorough cleaning of kitchen closets, cellar, etc., baking, etc.

Some housekeepers prefer to have washing done on Tuesday, thus securing Monday for a general brushing up and putting away after Sunday. If there are several children, or if you live in the country, and have city visitors from Saturday to Monday, you will find this free Monday a great boon. For although thorough sweeping once a week will allow no accumulation of dust in rooms that do not require it daily, if you have rugs and dark floors, they will look very much brighter and fresher for washing up on Monday morning, which if the washing is on hand there will be less chance of doing. Another case in which Tuesday for washing is an advantage, is when your servant is so slow or careless that she will let it hang on hand, unless pressure of other work hastens her.

Some one will say just here, " But if you are a good housekeeper, will you allow that ? "

I answer, " That would depend on circumstances."

In the present condition of things in this country we cannot hope for servants that are entirely satisfactory, and if I had one who suited me in many ways, yet who was incorrigible on that one point, I should think very seriously whether I could better put up with that fault than some others ; the pros and cons would have to be carefully weighed (and there will always be cons). But we must guard against another error. While avoiding a hasty dismissal of a fairly good servant for one or two faults, be careful not to retain one whose virtues and faults are so equally divided that she wears out your nerves and patience. You are better without assistance at all. Yet some of us do " put up with the ills we know, rather than rush into those we know not," and it is only when we have made the break, and parted with our " half treasure " we realize what an incubus is removed, how foolish we were.

To return to the Monday question. There are some serious objections to the free Monday. In the first place, servants almost invariably object to Tuesday washing and although you may, and would if you had good reason, insist on setting the day, independent of custom, should it happen that Tuesday is wet, the ironing is thrown late in the week and interferes with other work. Another drawback is, that then you have not Wednesday, which is the day on which any extra work can well be done—preserving, trying experiments in cooking, or doing any of the things that on busy days there is no time for. Where the house is small, all the sweeping can be done on Friday, and Thursday is then also an off day, but very often it is better to divide the sweeping, doing part on Thursday. For the purpose of this article, I will suppose that you are a novice in housekeeping and have a new servant and that it is Monday or "washing morning."

Before beginning the day's work it may be well to say that if you have been wise, you have arranged for an easily cooked breakfast. For instance, in winter substitute some quickly made hot bread—if it is necessary in your family—for hot cakes which take time to bake, in cold weather when mornings are shortest and food keeps well, a nice hash or stew or some scolloped fish can be prepared ready on Saturday, and will need only heating over. In summer it might be a rule to have Scotch eggs, or eggs poached on toast, with fruit, and oatmeal or mush on Mondays.

If the washing is large most housekeepers find it best, if they have only one servant, unless circumstances interfere, to give some assistance on Monday morning and will wash up the breakfast china and put it away, arrange the bedrooms, etc., but where the family is small and no such assistance is given, the breakfast things should nevertheless be washed and put away *at once*, not, as Delia loves to do—left on the kitchen table until the washing is on the line. Delia's argument is specious, she does not want to stop in her wash, she wants to get through, and, she is right so far, but if the family is small, the few dishes will not take ten minutes, and that ten minutes will be more than made up by the pleasure of working with clear table, and a clear mind. The same thing applies to the kitchen. Make it a rule that the kitchen be swept *every morning* before breakfast, and mats and carpets shaken. Too often on washing day everything that can be left is left, till the wash is over and the whole morning the kitchen (supposing you have no laundry) is kept untidy, and Delia herself although she doesn't understand the fact, is influenced by the state of things. She hurries to "get through," and the unkempt look makes her feel that she has a mountain of work ahead of her. While if she had spent ten minutes before breakfast in sweeping and ten after in clearing up, she would work at ease, and washing day would not be dreaded so much.

For Delia's sake and your own then, begin this first day that she is with you, and make her understand that although it is Monday you require the usual work to be done. Of course your judgment will tell you if such requirement is unreasonable. If there is a large wash, of course she should be allowed to get at it as early as possible, but in that case, it should be you who would do what she cannot do.

Any such innovation required from Delia, after she has settled down with you will be resisted, declared impossible, etc., therefore begin gently but firmly as you mean to continue. Do this in all things. There is no greater mistake in housekeeping than to make things smooth at first, with the idea of conciliating

Delia's opinion. When she learns afterwards what is really required, although it may be modest enough, she will feel imposed upon ; she will see, too, that you deprecate her discontent and unless she is very exceptional will take advantage of that fact.

Now we will return to Monday morning. Six o'clock is a good hour for Delia to leave her room in winter, any earlier hour is not advisable even on Monday, but in spring and summer five o'clock is not too early on that day, that the water may be hot, and all ready to begin washing in good time. She must be told to throw open her bed and open the window of her room top and bottom before leaving it. Also to go into parlor and dining room at once and in winter to open an inch or two of the top and bottom of one window in each room, to throw open shutters, draw up shades, open draft of stove, close dampers and shake it down. This *before* she lights her kitchen fire, as the rooms will air and the fire draw up meanwhile.

MANAGEMENT OF STOVES.

If the fire in a stove has plenty of fresh coals on top, not yet burnt through, it will need only a little shaking to start it up. But if the fire looks dying and the coals look white, *don't shake it.* When it has drawn till it is red again, if there is much ash and little fire, put coals on very carefully. A mere handful of fire can be coaxed back to life by adding another handful or so of *new* coals on the red spot, and giving plenty of draught, *but don't shake* a dying fire, or you lose it. This management is often necessary after a warm spell, when the stove has been kept dormant for days, and though I mention it this Monday morning, when I ought to be talking of other things, I hope you will not be so unfortunate as to have a fire to *coax* up on a cold winter morning. They should be arranged over night, so that all that is required is to open the draughts in order to have a cheery glow in a few minutes. This night work will be explained elsewhere.

THE KITCHEN FIRE.

In pursuance of my intention to leave no margin for what you may or may not know, we will begin with building the kitchen fire. For, although your maid *may* know how to get a mass of ignited coal in the stove, she may be far from knowing how to build a fire that will burn up brightly and *quickly*, which has a great deal to do with getting to work easily and successfully.

The average servant will assure you she knows how to make the fire, and she will almost certainly make it her own way, notwithstanding any directions you may give her. The first morning a new servant comes to you, rise with her. You need not wound her *amour propre* by assuming that she does not know her work. You may have chanced on a really competent woman, when, by all means, let well alone ; but there will be every reason for you to go down with her to the kitchen, to show the places of things, and if you have learned to make the fire yourself in the following way, and know the reasons for it being the best, you will, perhaps, by explaining these reasons, as you go on, be able to convince her. I doubt the ductility of her convictions, but if she is a girl worth keeping, she will at least consent to follow "your way," if it has been *shown* to her. Should she happily show such general intelligence about the fire as to make your interference needless, think yourself lucky, and store up your knowledge for another time.

All unnecessary interference with a servant's mode of work is to be avoided; always give her an opportunity for using what knowledge she has.

Perhaps it will help the entirely inexperienced housewife if I describe the wrong way to make a fire, or rather one of the several wrong ways.

The ashes from yesterday's fire are dumped without any precaution to avoid dust, the grate returned to its place, covers removed and, while the clouds of ashes belch forth into the kitchen, a quantity of paper is put in, and then a quantity of sticks; perhaps the first dozen are laid in straight, one on the other, flat on the paper, the rest tumbled in any how. Now that first layer of wood is pressing on the paper, and as entirely preventing any draught as if the wood were one thick stick. If the fire so built lights at all, it will be from the paper round the sides catching some of the smaller pieces of wood that were thrown on pell-mell. But this fire will light *slowly,* for you must remember there is always that mass at the bottom, preventing the draught from beneath, which will not itself ignite until the fire around is well established.

If, for experiment, you were to put out the slow flames, and take that fire apart, you would find a mass of paper at the bottom, burned all round to the very edge of the wood pressing on it, but where the wood has rested it will not even be discolored ; the wood will only be smoked outside and charred at the edges. Unless you are very enthusiastic you will not do this, and we are supposing that you do not do this, and that the upper pieces of wood have caught, as they may do if very dry. The average fire maker will now throw on heavily, from the scuttle, a quantity of coals, —perhaps fill up the stove. The flames are half quenched, the wood not sufficiently burned to make a foundation of glowing embers, may struggle to retain life, but that fire will not heat water for an hour ; the stove will be cool enough to put your hand on it for some time after you have put on the coals.

Now if the fire is made in the right way the result will be very different.

THE RIGHT WAY TO BUILD A FIRE.

Remove the covers, brush all the dust and ashes from the inside top of the stove into the grate, replace the covers, close all the draughts, and, if your range has a dust valve, open it. Then gently dump the contents of the grate, and wait a few seconds to let the dust subside. Put shavings or plenty of crumpled-up newspaper (never use folded paper or pamphlets unless they are torn asunder and *crumpled singly*) into the grate. Then lay on the paper some light sticks, *crossing them*, letting some rest against the side of the grate to support the others, so that they do not press on the paper. Use sufficient wood. There is no economy in stinting it, yet, where it has to be bought for kindling, there must be no waste. Much depends on the kind of wood, but as a rule you let the wood come to the tops of the bricks. Then light the paper, having first opened the draughts. While the wood kindles, put on the washboiler (unless you have hot water attachments) and fill the water tank, if it is not self-filling. Rinse out the kettle, fill it with fresh water and set it on the stove. When the wood is *well burnt up,*— not when the flames are merely licking the outside of the sticks, but when you have a *good wood fire,*—throw on, gently, only enough coals to just cover the wood. Your range will be hot all over from the wood fire. Putting on only a few coals at a time will not check it much, while your kettle, oven, and water, are all getting hot.

The wrong way, as I have said, is to pour on nearly a scuttleful of coals at first, smothering the wood, and this will take a long time to burn up, while the fire made as I have directed is a good fire *from the beginning.* The few coals leave room for a fierce draught, and your oven will be ready for baking in a very few minutes. While these few coals are burning up, take away the ashes and sift them. If you have a covered sifter fixed on a barrel it will not be five minutes work to do it at once. The cinders should be put right from the sifter into a scuttle and carried back to the kitchen, to be used during the day. Then if the coals are nearly burned through throw on more, not many.

After the ashes are taken up, brush them off the range neatly into a dustpan, then quickly go over it with a blacklead brush, or a cloth kept for the purpose. Once a week it needs thorough blacking.

If it is winter there will be fires in other rooms to attend to. As the draughts were regulated when you first came down, they will now be ready for coals or further shaking down. If there is a carpet under the stove, lay a newspaper down and take up the ashes quickly and neatly, brush off the stove as you did the kitchen range, always keeping a separate brush for the kitchen.

This business of lighting fire, taking up ashes and sifting them need only take a very short time in the doing. A bright girl will see that while the fire is burning up, she can get the ashes from the kitchen taken up, and when the coal is first put on, before the stove gets too hot, she will go over it with brush and rag, fitting one piece of work into the other; so that she will have no minutes of waiting. When the fires are attended to, she will perhaps need to put on oatmeal or mush, for which the water will now be boiling ; or prepare anything for breakfast which will require long cooking; then she will sweep the kitchen and piazzas, shaking mats, etc. If briskly done, a quarter of an hour will suffice, for the last. If it is winter the lighting fire, attending to stove, and taking up ashes, etc., may take half an hour. We will assume, then, that it is a quarter to seven, your fire bright, mush or oatmeal on the fire, and kitchen and piazzas swept. If you have breakfast at half-past seven, whether there will be time to go into the parlor and set that in order, will depend on the kind of breakfast ; but the dining-room must always be neat. If kept so regularly, five minutes will dust it and remove anything that should not be in it, before laying the cloth, which now do carefully.

At seven, make any quick biscuit. (I am supposing you have an easy breakfast, as it is washing morning.) Put them in the oven, grind the coffee, set the milk to get hot at back of the stove, so that you can bring it forward the last thing and let it boil. If you put it in a very hot spot at first you must watch it or it will boil over, and sometimes be in danger of scorching. If you have potatoes to warm over, do them now ; if not, you should have put some in the oven when you put the mush to cook. Half an hour to forty minutes will bake them. Now make the coffee and poach or boil eggs, or broil the ham, and serve breakfast. Let me here say that coffee should never be made until the last thing ; it loses fragrance by standing, yet it is quite a common practice to make the coffee when the mush is put on to cook.

While the family is at breakfast the soiled water may be brought down stairs, and then the clothes be sorted for the wash, unless this has been done the day before.

I am aware many will say on washing morning I have indicated too many things to do ; that surely the piazza might be left unswept, or the dining-room undusted, the slops unemptied,—at least till the first boilerful of clothes was on the fire,—but, after long experience and trial of the several ways, I do not think much time is actually gained by leaving these trifles, and, as I have before pointed out, the feeling of comfort with which the work is done amply repays the lost time. If the few things that add so much to the family comfort are neglected through the morning, in order to get to the washing, you will not save half an hour ; that is to say, your clothes may not be out to dry till half an hour later ; if the wash is small, this will matter little ; if large, one pair of hands probably will not be depended upon for all. Where there is a servant, if one thing is allowed to be neglected because it is washing morning, everything will gradually be expected to yield to the same necessity, and even the ashes not taken up, or any but the kitchen fire regulated.

Where the family is more than two the dusting and bed making should certainly be done by some member of the family on washing day, but while avoiding all *extra* work on that day, and planning to have easily cooked meals, do not run, as many women do into the other extreme, and allow Monday to be a day of general discomfort and hurry skurry ; with cold meat and hasty service at meals ; there is no reason for it. In the same household I have known a capable servant to manage her work so that the washing made no difference to any one's comfort, and she who did it was neat, and unhurried ; everything went on Monday as any other day, and her ironing was up stairs as soon as that of the wild, hurrying, panting girls, for whom Monday had seemed a day of slavery, who had preceded and who followed her.

Where no servant is kept, and a woman is called in to do washing, the housewife will find no advantage in leaving any of the usual work necessary to the comfort of the family undone. Care should be taken however, that the top of the range is left as free as possible and the oven used so far as may be for cooking the dinner.

PROGRAMME OF WORK.

Under this head will be given with each instalment the special work for the day, and ways of doing it told briefly for hasty reference with fuller explanation of methods and reasons for them in " Progressive Housekeeping." This does not imply that the one is merely an enlargement or repetition of the other. As all women of experience know, recipes or methods of work should be as direct and little complicated as possible with outside details, if they are to be easily grasped by the tyro. And yet the woman who knows the why and wherefore of her work will do it intelligently and successfully ; while if she does not know the reasons for working in a certain way, that way may seem very new fangled or unnecessary. To avoid, however, the useless and wearisome repetition of giving with each part the work that is *daily* required in every house, it is given once for all under the head of *"general* early morning work for every winter day." The *special* work for each day of the week will be given, each with its own instalment.

EARLY MORNING WORK FOR EVERY WINTER DAY.

On coming down in the morning, raise shades in all rooms, open blinds, close dampers, and open the draughts in all stoves. If the fires are bright and good put on coal ; if dull, wait until they brighten before either shaking them or adding fuel.

Make kitchen fire ; (See full directions in Chapter I) rinse and fill the kettle, boiler, etc.

Take up ashes ; sweep kitchen and corridors—beating all mats.

If the fires have now come up in other rooms, open one window an inch or two—top and bottom, then put on coals, shake the ashes out (unless there is very little fire in the stove, when it will be wise to put on only a small quantity of coal at first, and do not disturb by shaking until the fresh coal has taken fire).

Take up ashes, brush the stoves neatly. If you have no time to blacken them, rub them over with a rag to remove the white, dusty look the ashes leave.

If the morning is very cold do not leave the windows open many minutes ; ten will renew the air.

When the kitchen fire has burned up, place near it any buckwhat cakes or risen biscuit you may want for breakfast ; bake potatoes, make corn bread, or in short, prepare whatever will take longest to cook.

Grind coffee, lay the cloth for breakfast, assure yourself that fires are progressing well, close draughts of those sufficiently hot, open dampers if needful.

After breakfast, clear the table and brush up crumbs if necessary.

Wash breakfast dishes and put them away, setting aside steel knives after they are washed, to clean in the following way:

TO CLEAN STEEL KNIVES.

Have a smooth piece of board and bath brick. Rub the brick on the board which is better than to scrape it with a knife; the rubbing grinds the brick easily and quickly into fine powder. Now, hold the knife firmly by the haft and rub it swiftly from one end of the board to the other, (not as is usually done by pushing it *to* and *from* you). There is some art in cleaning knives in this way, but once you are used to it, you will be well repaid by the fact that they have always a brilliant polish like a new knife, and are always sharp. The first time knives are so cleaned they may take some time before you get the same degree of brightness all over. Freeing them from all stain first with sapolio will help; then the blade must be held lightly but *evenly* on the board. There is no hard labor about it, only an easy swinging of the arm back and forth. After once cleaning in this way, if done every day, there will be no further trouble. When the knives are brilliant and without any dark shadows, dust them with a *dry* duster (do not wash them) taking care to free the handles from every trace of brick dust.

Now, proceed to bedroom work. If the morning is very cold, and the windows have been open an inch or two, top and bottom, since the occupant left the room, with mattress turned back and pillows airing, they may now be closed, unless there is a stove in the room, where they should be left open as much as possible except in the severest weather. Remove soiled water, wash soap dish, fold towels—changing when necessary, then make up the bed. If a stove is in the room, it should receive attention, ashes being removed and the whole dusted before the general work of the room is begun. If in consequence of a fire the windows are left open, close the door of the room on leaving it that the cool air may be confined to that one room. The chamber work over and stairs swept down, trim, clean, and fill lamps, and then proceed to the special work for the day.

CHAPTER III.

I HAVE spoken of making some quick biscuit for breakfast. I have not given the recipe, nor do I think it will be necessary to give many cooking recipes in this series of papers. The chances are that you have a good cookery book, if not, it will be wise to get one, but here let me say a word : There are four or five excellent and reliable books in the market, the names of whose writers are guarantee of their excellence, and they are worth everything to a young housekeeper, because you may be quite sure if you fail with one of these recipes, you have but to try again, the fault will be yours, not that of the writer; but if you take one of the dozens of fugitive recipes, that are scattered through newspapers, the chances are that you will meet with vexation and disappointment; an experienced cook might make some use of them, for she would see at a glance wherein they lacked, the vague and sometimes wrong directions would be supplemented by her own knowledge of what must be right, but it is very seldom that anything is published in this irresponsible way which cannot be found *precisely* and *correctly* given in a standard work. In the same way, in buying a cookery book, do not be beguiled by a cheap compilation from some obscure publishing house, which is generally made up of the newspaper recipes before alluded to. Of course, in speaking of newspaper recipes, I do not mean those written expressly for them by the best qualified women in the country. These and the recipes which appear in Good Housekeeping, of course, have the gurantee of the author's name, and anything not perfectly clear can be enquired for. But, although I do not intend to give recipes in this series, which would swell it beyond due limits, I do intend to say, on the subject of cooking, that which may make it more easy to manage.

The best plan in small, plain families, for a Monday dinner, is so to provide that there will be cold meat to warm over, and the warming over need not necessarily be hash or stew. If care is taken not to over cook a roast on Sunday, and it is carved fairly and evenly (and by all means learn enough of the art of carving to compass this), lay it flat on a drippingpan, cover it well with dripping from the day before, not the *gravy;* keep that to warm separately, and put it in a very hot oven at a quarter past twelve o'clock for a one o'clock meal; at half past, put potatoes to boil, and a few minutes later, peas, beans, asparagus, cauliflower or cabbage. Always put any fresh vegetable in boiling water. Beets or carrots should be put on to boil at twelve and turnips at a quarter past. If you make it understood in your kitchen that vegetables take a certain time, make that time known and insist on it being remembered, there will be fewer spoiled vegetables. Also remember that the vegetables are to be ruled by the meat. Take pains to understand your oven, and you will soon learn how long the sized piece of meat required by your family will take to roast, then let the vegetables be cooked according to the following table:

TIME TABLE FOR BOILING VEGETABLES.

Potatoes, half an hour, unless small, when rather less.

Peas and asparagus twenty to twenty-five minutes.

Cabbage and cauliflower, twenty-five minutes to half an hour.

String beans, if slit or sliced slantwise and thin, twenty-five minutes; if only snapped across, forty minutes.

Green corn, twenty to twenty-five minutes.

Lima beans, if very young, half an hour, old, forty to forty-five minutes.

Carrots and turnips, forty-five minutes when young, one hour to one and a half in winter.

Beets, one hour in summer, one hour and half, or two hours, in winter. Very large ones take four hours.

Onions, medium size, one hour.

RULE.—*All vegetables to go into fast boiling water to be quickly brought to the boiling point again,* not left to steep in the hot water before boiling which *wilts* them and destroys color and flavor.

This time table must always be regulated by the hour at which the meat will be done. If the meat should have to wait five minutes for the vegetables, there will be a loss of punctuality, but the dinner will not be damaged ; but if the vegetables are done, and wait for the meat, your dinner will certainly be much the worse, yet so general is the custom of over-boiling vegetables or putting them to cook in a haphazard way, somewhere *about* the time, that very many people would not recognize the damage; they would very quickly see the superiority of vegetables just cooked the right time, but would attribute it to some superiority in the article itself, that they were fresher, and finer, not knowing that the finest and freshest, improperly cooked, are little better than the poor ones.

I am led to dwell on this point of vegetable cooking, because it is so general to find them spoiled, when all else is well cooked. How many of us will recognize the familiar reply of unpunctual servants, when asked why dinner is not served, "The vegetables were all done, but not the meat."

I repeat, the meat must be the standard, and that it may be so, and dinner not a movable feast, always see that the oven and fire are arranged for baking one hour before your meat is to go in; meat put into a cool oven is never well cooked and, in summer, quite spoiled.

Perhaps I should say, in this connection, that after breakfast the fire should be made up,—that is, coals thrown on as far as the top of the bricks, not higher, or it will choke, the draughts closed, and then it can be left until, say eleven, for a one o'clock meal (unless a large joint is to be cooked, when as much earlier as necessary). At eleven, or earlier, rake the ashes out, open the draughts, and see that everything is favorable to making a hot fire ; when nearly red at the top, showing the coals have all burned through, shut off some part of the draught, so that the fire may not exhaust itself by drawing up the chimney. Should it have become a fiercely glowing mass almost at white heat, the coals are almost exhausted already, the draughts have been open too long. Sprinkle on a thin layer of coals, just to cover the red; it will not check the oven, but simply give something to burn on, otherwise having once attained the white heat point, it would begin to die off just as you need its strength.

If the fire is required for ironing, or other purposes, be careful to put on a few coals before you leave the kitchen after cooking dinner and leave it solid for the afternoon, but on days when no fire is required until the tea, burn up all the garbage from the vegetables. Potato peelings, pea shucks, etc., burn splendidly if put on a hot fire. Put no coals over them, or they will choke and smother, open all draughts so that the odor may go up the chimney, and after dinner they will be consumed and leave a glowing mass of embers, on which you throw a few coals or cinders and close up the stove as you did after breakfast.

I have dwelt very long on the management of the kitchen fire, knowing how very much easy housekeeping depends on it, and how few servants understand it, and how unlikely the inexperienced housekeeper, to whom these papers may be chiefly useful, is to do so.

I will say here a few words about washing, although the directions will be fully given in the programme of work. In addition to those directions I would say that they are given for those who have no such advantages as stationary tubs, washing machines, etc., although, of course, the facts hold good where you have them. See that everything is as convenient as possible for the worker; the wash bench suited to a short woman will try the back of a tall one, yet I have known such a one quite unable to arrange anything better for herself. A box or board will often make the difference necessary. See that the washboard is not worn, or it will tear clothes and hands.

There are various ways of washing. Many soak clothes over night, others think if the extra time it takes to soak them and to wring them out be considered, that there is no gain. I am inclined to agree with this view unless the clothes are much soiled. You will please yourself which method you adopt, also as to whether you will put a tablespoonful of borax into the tub or one of turpentine, or simply rub soap on the soiled parts. The thing there is *no* choice about, is the proper sorting of clothes, this and abundance of water is the secret of the pearly clearness that distinguishes some laundry work. After separating flannels and colored things, put handkerchiefs, collars, and all the finer articles by themselves, also table cloths and napkins, sheets, pillow cases, etc.

About the making of starch there are so many opinions that I can but give the methods, and let each try for herself. Some experienced women say there is no necessity for boiling the starch, but that it should be made like cocoa; that is, a small quantity should be wetted in as little cold water as will make a thin, smooth paste, then pour on it, slowly, actually boiling water—stirring all the time—till there are no white streaks or any cloudiness in it; it will be thick and clear, and the absence of white shows that the boiling water has cooked all the starch.   I have seen excellent laundry work in which the starch has been made thus. The more usual way is to make the starch in the same way, pour boiling water on it till it thickens, and then set it on the range to boil.   Some say it should boil long, others very little.   I only know, that for the most beautiful ironing I ever saw, the starch was always boiled a very long time, an hour or so, sometimes more, till it fell from the spoon like clear white syrup, and on asking the woman what caused the beautiful clearness of her nainsooks and lawns, the peculiar soft stiffness, which differed so much from the paper-like texture of any one else's work, if equally stiff:

"It's just the boiling of the starch ma'am, and that causes all the sticking to the iron, and when it isn't half boiled the clothes muss as soon as you get them on."

I had noticed that her clothes, beside looking so well, had the quality of not getting tumbled so soon. I, therefore, in my own house, adopt the method of boiling the starch very long.

The laundress above alluded to, used nothing in the starch except for collars and thick materials, when she used borax, but she was a very expert and experienced ironer.   A teaspoonful of borax to half a gallon of boiled starch, is undoubtedly a help to the worker and helps the clothes to retain stiffness. A small piece of lard or wax is preferred by some, salt by others. The reason against using the latter, I think, is this: Salt, as is well known, attracts moisture, and in damp weather clothes so starched are more likely to get limp. Well made starch helps the ironing immensely, yet nothing but practice will make a good ironer.

Table linen should be very slightly starched. The starch through which all the fine things have passed may be further thinned and used for pillow cases and table linen.

Another thing that helps the ironing is neat folding and *close*, fine sprinkling. The clothes should be brought in from the line, then each piece sprinkled, For a few cents you can buy a sprinkler which will save the heavy splashes alternated with large dry spaces which results from inexperienced hand sprinkling. You may fold each towel, and pillow case lengthwise, as you intend to iron it, or you may think it easier to lay several of each kind on the other, roll them up together and fold when you iron. Table-cloths or sheets require two persons when possible. They should be folded with great care in half from end to end, and then fold the half again in the same direction. You have now folded it in four lengthwise. I mention this particularly, although I have no doubt most ladies know that they should be so folded, but I must remind my readers that I am allowing no margin for what may be already known.

If your irons have not been lately used, or if you find trouble in cleaning them, wash them thoroughly in soap and water with a brush; this should be done every two or three weeks, for irons get soiled by standing on the range when in use and on the shelves when not, and although the face of them will look clean and bright, black specks fall from the upper part, or where pushed up into the gathers, there will often remain the mark of the "nose" of the iron. To wash them, let them get a little warm on the range, then put them in a dishpan of hot water and scrub them, setting them on the range to dry.

The iron holder should be well made, comfortable to the hand, and have slip-covers of ticking, or linen, which can be slipped off and washed every week or so.

PROGRAMME OF WORK.

SPECIAL WORK FOR MONDAY—WASHING.

Have all ready before you begin to work. Sort the clothes, separating the shirts, collars and starched white things generally from the bed linen, towels and flannels, and separate these again from coarser things.

FLANNELS.—The main thing with flannel is quick drying, and that they be *washed* and *rinsed* in water of the *same temperature* very quickly, and not allowed to cool between. To accomplish this, wash one article at a time, putting it into warm soapy water. (Many good housekeepers say *hot* water, and if you have only one or two articles to wash that will do; but if you have several, they will chill and shrink before they get into the second water).

Do not rub flannels on a board; the dirt so easily comes out of woolen goods that it is needless, and ruins the texture; wash them quickly and thoroughly through one water, wring them and wash them through a second water in which you may have a little bluing (for white ones); this second water must be the *same temperature as the first;* wring them, shake them well and hang them out *immediately* to dry.

Colored flannels must never be washed after white, or they will be covered when dry with lint. Flannels are best washed first, because they should have water for themselves; the second water from them will do nicely for the first of your white clothes.

Wash the finer white things and so on until you come to the coarse. Put few pieces in the tub at a time so that you always have abundance of water, which if your tub is stuffed nearly full you cannot have. Drop them as you do them into a tub of warm water, wash them through that and put them in the boiler (soap ing all discolored parts) with plenty of cold water Let them come to the boiling point; they will be no whiter for long boiling. Take them out with a stout clothes stick, and drop them into clear water, wash thoroughly, turning each piece wrong side out, then wring them out of this (after you have put more clothes in the boiler) and put them into water made slightly blue, with ball bluing tied tightly in a piece of flannel. Wring them from the blue water after rinsing them thoroughly; hang out those pieces at once which are not to be starched. The others pass through hot starch, doing those first which require to be most stiff. Shake them well after they are wrung out, and hang to dry.

The water through which you passed the clothes from the boiler will do for the colored things, as it will only be soapy, not soiled. Many keep the flannels and use this water to "first" them.

COLORED CLOTHES. — Delicate colors should be quickly washed in warm soapy water rinsed without bluing, and hung *in the shade* to dry. Many colors that stand the water will fade when drying under the sun.

TO SET THE COLOR IN BLUE LAWN OR CALICO.— Dissolve three cents' worth of saltpetre in a pail of water and dip the articles in several times before washing.

TO SET ANY DOUBTFUL COLORS. — Dissolve ten cents' worth of sugar of lead in two pails of water; soak the articles in it, then wash.

I have an amendment to add, to both these recipes, which I give as they are written. I *know* the sugar of lead sets the color; even the tenderest blue will be safe, but, what sets the color *will set dirt.* Therefore grievous as it is to wet a lawn before wearing, soak it in the piece before it is made up. (Why does not the maker do this?)

I have given above the regulation method of washing, but the boiling, especially in summer, is not necessary. By using a little borax in the water, which is quite harmless and will brighten most colors, and thorough washing *and rinsing,* the clothes will be even whiter without boiling, and much time and labor saved. Stains from perspiration should have soap rubbed on them and be laid in the hot sun.

To TAKE OUT STAINS.—Every housekeeper should examine the table linen for fruit stains which will become fixed if they are put into suds.

Place the stain over a bowl and pour *boiling* water through it from the kettle; it will remove it at once.

To TAKE OUT INK AND IRON MOULD WITHOUT CHEMICALS.—Wet the spot with lemon juice, sprinkle it with salt, and lay it in the sun. You may need to repeat this two or three times.

To REMOVE MACHINE OIL STAINS.—Before putting newly made clothes into the wash, look at the hems and tucks for oil stains; rub all spots or dark stitching with soap and cold water; it will come out very easily. If put into hot suds before this is done, it may be permanently stained.

Articles requiring to be very stiff, should be starched twice, once with boiled starch after they are rinsed and before hanging to dry, and with raw starch when dry.

To MAKE STARCH.—Make the boiled starch with three tablespoonfuls of starch to a quart of water and half a teaspoonful of borax.

When dry take in clothes, and if possible, iron the flannels at once; iron them on the wrong side with a cool iron until quite dry. Sprinkle the clothes carefully and fold them. (See remarks.)

Starch collars, cuffs, etc., again with raw starch.

Be careful about folding shirts and night gowns after starching, as nothing is more disagreeable than patches of starch on parts where it is not intended to be.

Fold shirt or gown lengthwise so that the two starched fronts come together, lay the wrist bands between them, then roll up very tight, sprinkling the rest of the garment with water.

Pack all the clothes closely in the basket, **cover** with a damp cloth and then a dry one until **ready to iron.**

CHAPTER IV.

BED-ROOM WORK, AND IRONING.

IN small families, say of three persons, in fine drying weather, the greater part of the ironing may be done on Monday, and should, even in a large one be finished on Tuesday.

Space did not allow me, in speaking of the Monday routine, to give details of bed-room work. It is perhaps needless to say that, on leaving the room in the morning, the windows should be thrown open, top and bottom, the pillows put on the sill to air, and the sheets also. The mattress should be half turned over and left so until the bed is made up. In some very, very neat houses, especially in the country, the beds are made up very early. I have known the girls of a family to be brought up to make their beds before they leave the room. It looks neat and nice to leave a chamber in perfect order, but it is not a healthy custom. A bed requires at least an hour to air it. During the night exhalations from the skin pass into the bedclothes (I am afraid to say how much these exhalations weigh, according to science, but it is something much larger than the unscientific mind can easily take in). If these bedclothes are thoroughly aired in the hot sun or wind, they pass out, but this cannot happen if the bed is made up again a few minutes after occupation, the mattress, in fact, still warm from it. This so-called very neat and tidy habit of anti-breakfast bed-making is, therefore, an unclean one. For myself, in warm weather, I think the bed of an adult should be left a couple of hours before being made up.

But I am not advocating the other uncomfortable extreme of leaving the beds unmade till late. The housekeeper who does her own work will find it best to bring down the water even before washing breakfast dishes or arranging the front of her house for the day, which, as I have pointed out, she may find it advisable to do, even before the necessary work in the kitchen, and after the breakfast is cleared and the dishes washed, the first thing should be the beds.

The mattress should be turned over entirely, sometimes, from head to foot, at others, from side to side, so as to vary the pressure and keep it even. There should be an " under blanket " to lay over the mattress, but there are some young housekeepers of limited means who may not have, in winter, blankets to spare for this purpose, but it saves the tick very much to have in its place an old soft quilt, or any other article that is easily aired. Physicians recommend the use of an old blanket, because it is woolen and both absorbs perspiration without giving chill, and, also, being so porous, is more easily aired than cotton. The use of this extra cover to the mattress is twofold,— sanitary and economical; sanitary, because it is so much more easy to purify in the air than the mattress itself, and economical, because the tick of a mattress so treated will last twice the time, fresh and clean, than one only covered with a sheet will do. This first covering should be drawn smoothly over the mattress and tucked in under it; the under sheet, with the broad hem at the top, should come next, and should be large enough to admit of being firmly tucked round the mattress. Nothing is more unpleasant than to find, during the night, that the under sheet has slipped down and we are lying on the mattress.

Bolster covers, although not really necessary where the sheets are very long and the bolster can be rolled in it, are yet a great convenience and assistance to neat bed making. The bolster of course, follows the sheet, is laid evenly upon it, and the superfluous fullness tucked smoothly under it. See to the foot of the bed first, tucking it all evenly along, so that it will not readily come out at night, using only enough of the sheet for the purpose; then lay your hand along the sheet below the bolster, lay the sheet smoothly over the latter, and take care that the whole is perfectly straight and the center fold in the middle of the bed; lay on the blanket and quilt, tuck all in neatly, but not too tightly; turn the sheet over once about five inches, and then again making the fold very even and smooth. There are two or three modes of turning down the sheet, some preferring to leave it unturned, and to lay the pillow upon it. Let every one do as they please; the one thing necessary to good bed-making is that each article be laid on without wrinkles or folds, and well tucked in, the rest is a matter of taste.

The pillows should be pressed flat from the center with both hands (after being well shaken); this will make them stand up well. Although pillow and sheet shams add very much to the appearance of a bed, I confess I do not like them, simply because they are shams. I prefer the old-time ruffled pillow cases, the ruffle of lawn or nainsook all round, and simply ironed, not fluted, in the graceful, simple fashion of our grandmothers.

The bed made, the room should be lightly brushed up if necessary (and for such bits as gather during a day, the sweeper is invaluable), dusted, set in order, and darkened during the heat of the day. The stairs and corridor should be brushed and then, perhaps, you will be ready to begin ironing, or finish what may have been left undone from yesterday.

For making the fire for ironing, rake out all ashes and get it up by putting on coals and leaving draughts open. *Take care not to over fill* the fire-box, or it will choke. Many otherwise good laundresses, do not understand the fire ; that is, they are quite capable of making the fire up, and creating a fiery furnace for the time being, but before the ironing is finished the fire is down, irons "won't heat," and then the remedy is wood, and wood is either burned for the rest of the day, or the last things ironed are done in that miserable limp fashion that results from using half cold irons.

The fire should be carefully kept up, which is very easily done without in the least checking the heat if, every hour or so, a little coal is added on one side.

The irons, if necessary, may be shifted to the hot side until the other has burned through, and then the other may be likewise replenished. Care should be taken, also to keep the bottom free from ashes. The general rule among servants seems to be to make the fire as large and hot as possible at the beginning, and then to iron vigorously so long as it lasts; some who have not acquired the bad habit of trusting to wood to bring up the fire (one of the most incurable of bad kitchen habits I have found it to be), and do somewhat better than the average, will yet iron till the fire goes down, then put on a quantity of coal, and while it is burning up leave the ironing till the irons are again hot. This is not so bad as using the fire without replenishing till past redemption, but it is far better not to let it go down at all. The cause of the mistake is the false idea that adding coals will check the fire. It will do so, if you wait till it is getting poor, but a few coals put on to a fierce fire from time to time, will make little difference.

This matter of thoroughly understanding the kitchen fire may be thought to occupy undue space in these papers, but the whole comfort of the house may be said to hinge on it. This may seem an extreme thing to say, but every housekeeper knows what a difference there is in the kitchen fire that is always ready, and the one that is always *un*ready. The latter always "has just got fresh coal on," or "was good a quarter of an hour ago,"—in short, is never hot when wanted and always so when there is no need of it. In the first case there is always hot water, a hot iron at five minutes' notice, a cup of hastily made tea for a visitor, or an extra dish can be improvised,—in short, that fire is always ready for the emergency, the other never is, and failures, lack of patience, fatigue and general mild misery are the result.

For general work of each day see programme No. 1.

SPECIAL WORK FOR TUESDAY—IRONING.

Although, when the washing is small, part of the ironing may be done on Monday in good weather, yet, in a large majority of cases, it is Tuesday's work, and so we will treat it now.

The fire for ironing should be made up directly after breakfast, the stove being rubbed off with paper if it has become soiled with cooking the breakfast and irons set on to heat while the dishes are washed and bed-room work is being done.

Ironing is such clean work that either mistress or maid might put on their usual afternoon dress instead of remaining in working dress.

To IRON SHIRTS.—Iron the entire shirt first, then pass a cloth wrung from cold water over the bosom, lay under it a bosom board, draw the linen perfectly straight and take care to leave no wrinkles; if you iron them in, you have to moisten the spot and it rarely looks well after. Be careful to raise any plaits there may be with your iron, so that it does not remain plastered to the under surface; and, above all things, iron *until it is dry*.

This ironing each article until it is dry is very important, as it gives that smooth, crisp feeling to linen which shows the difference between good and bad ironing. If any article is put to air while damp it will dry rough.

POLISHING. — Polishing shirt bosoms and collars has gone out of use now very much, but if any one wishes to produce a glazed surface, all they have to do is to use a polishing iron and main strength.

Iron flannels on the wrong side, with an iron that barely sizzles under a wet finger, until they are quite dry.

For ironing sheets, pillow cases, towels, tablecloths, napkins, etc., fold lengthwise twice, then twice across. Always iron the way of the thread, or parallel with the selvedge.

Use a little wax tied in a coarse rag for your irons and have convenient a small board on which knife brick or fine ashes has been sprinkled, rub your iron on this, then dust thoroughly over and under with a large duster. Don't waste time in trying to iron with cool irons. Make up your fire, cover the irons with a large tin cover—a dish pan or wash boiler will do— and turn to something else, resolving to manage better next time.

Covering the irons, by concentrating the heat, saves time when the fire is low or if your doors or windows are so arranged as to blow on the stove. A sheet iron cover comes for the express purpose, but very good shift may be made as I have described.

Iron only the feet of ribbed stockings.

When the ironing is finished put away holders, dusters, and wax in a bag or box appropriated for them, air the boards, and put them away.

Fold all the clothes neatly as soon as aired and carry them up stairs.

CHAPTER V.

IRONS that have once been red hot, never retain the heat so well afterwards, and will always be rough; therefore, while losing no opportunity of using your fire, be careful not to put them on the stove hours before they are needed; and after using them, do not set them away flat on the floor or shelf, always stand them on end. When it is possible, have every really useful modern appliance, of which there are so many now-a-days, to make work easy. To the woman who has no assistance in her work, even a small expense may be looked upon as economy, if it saves strength; that unpurchasable thing of which young women are often so prodigal. I know, however, there are homes where true economy is recognized, and where a few dollars would not be grudged to lighten the wife's burden, yet if the dollars are not there how can it be done? Let us hope then, at least, the husband is handy with tools, and can make some things he cannot buy. That he can put a shelf just where she needs it, to save her holding a lamp, while she cooks the winter supper, and if he can make an ironing table which shall hold the necessaries for ironing, and when not in use form a seat, so much the better; but one thing not difficult to make, and which will save many a weary backache, is a seat exactly suited to the height of the woman needing it. All small things can just as well be ironed seated as standing, *if the seat be right*.

Many a tired woman takes a chair and makes up her mind she will iron the collars and small things, seated, but the resolution lasts only a moment, she is soon on her aching feet again, and then she believes she is too nervous to work in a sitting position. It is nothing of the kind, the seat is not adapted to the height of the table, and she really finds herself working at such disadvantage for her arms, that mechanically she assumes the old position. Let *seat and table* be adjusted to her, and she will soon find ironing or making cake, or rolling out cookies quite as easily accomplished in sitting as standing. The seat must be high enough to bring her elbows well above the table, and give her the same command of it as if she were standing, and with this seat she would of course require a stool or box on which to rest the feet.

Such a seat will be of little use in cooking, without forethought to see that you have all your materials at hand before you begin to work. I know many an energetic woman with abundant strength will say: " Oh, I would not *sit* to work " and feel that it was a poor way of doing. But there are women less strong, perhaps who have lost the strength on which they once prided themselves, and will just as readily say: "If I only could manage to sit."

At first, it may seem that you have to jump up and down so often that you save little, but by degrees you will find the benefit, even if you only are enabled to sit five minutes out of twenty that you would otherwise stand, and as you get used to the sitting, you will be astonished to find how many things you can do sitting, and how little the jumping up that appeared so tiresome at first, will be needed when you have gotten used to providing against it. Many things we now stand to do, as I say, may be done seated, but I began to speak especially of ironing.

Most people, now-a-days, use the skirt board for ironing everything. It should be covered with three thicknesses of heavy flannel, an old blanket is best, but a comfortable can be made to do; over this securely baste part of an old sheet, or any white cotton cloth without seams, that you may prefer for the purpose. The bosom board should be covered in the same way, and the covers of both frequently changed,

CHAPTER VI.

I HAVE alluded before to the advisability of getting dishes washed and out of the way, now we will say something more definite about that so often dreaded task.

To do it pleasantly and easily you need two large dish pans, in one of which you have very hot water and soap, the other empty, and a tray at your right hand. Lay the silver in the hot water; at first you may find it difficult to bear your hands in it, but very soon it will be easy; use a mop to help you wash the silver, take it out, and lay in the empty dish pan, roll the glasses round in the hot water, and put them also in with the silver, then put the remainder of the china in the water. Take the kettle of boiling water and pour enough over glasses and silver to rinse them; take a clean dish towel, or glass cloth, and rolling each glass in the hot water, take it out at once and wipe it. It will be so hot that it will dry at once and take a high polish in a moment. Lay each glass when dried on a tray. Take out the silver, using a mop to assist; this also being hot almost dries itself, give each piece a vigorous rub with the dry cloth, lay it on the tray, and then return to the china.

Wash quickly and carefully to prevent chipping

the edges, lay each piece as you do it in the second dish pan, leaving greasy things till last. If you have not been interrupted and have worked quickly, your water will still be hot; if there is danger of it cooling while you wipe the silver and glass, set it on the stove before you begin. Use more soap with the greasy things. Your dish water should always be a hot lather, not half cold, greasy water, which leaves a dirty scum on hands and round the dish pan. When all the dishes are washed, pour boiling water from the kettle plentifully over them, then wipe them quickly from the hot water. Use this hot clean water for the tins, saucepans, or whatever you may afterwards have to wash.

As usually done, the wiping is a much longer business than the washing, because even people who use two waters take them out of the last "to drain," thinking then to lessen the wiping, but if they will try wiping each piece direct from the hot water, they will see that the rapid evaporation half does the work. Glass, silver, and china, so washed, is always brilliant; even delicate hands are not injured, and the work is clean and pleasant.

A word about saucepans. Do you know, and will you believe, that you may save all the labor of scraping saucepans in which oatmeal or mush has been boiled, by simply observing one precaution? Instead of taking it boiling from the fire, and pouring it out into the dish, let it stand on the table for five minutes, before you pour it from the saucepan. I do not mean that you are to leave it long enough to get cool; the mush and oatmeal porridge hold the heat so long, that five minutes away from the fire will make little perceptible difference except to the bottom of the saucepan. If you notice when you pour mush boiling from the saucepan, you will find the heat of the bottom instantly dries up what is left on. The usual way is to pour water to this and put it back on the stove; now the water will take hours to soak through the hard crust that coats the bottom of the saucepan, which, having been set back on the stove is baking still harder. When the mush is poured from the saucepan, after it has stood on a cool spot for a few minutes, you will find that the bottom is no longer baking hot, and if, for the sake of experiment, you take a spoon immediately, you will find the cake on the bottom will peel away and leave it clean.

You will not, however, want to do this while getting breakfast, except once by way of experiment, therefore you can pour water in the saucepan, and leave it either in the sink or, if you require the water warm, on a cool part of the stove. A large clam shell is far better than a knife or spoon to scrape pots.

I said put the saucepan on the table, and, lest I may seem regardless of the scrubbing it would cause, let me hasten to recommend a contrivance or two which will add much to your convenience; I mean the use of "pot boards." The simplest may be the bottom of a butter firkin or small keg, one or two of these with a hole and string through each kept hanging near the table, save many a dark mark or stain. A still better way, however, is to have a small square board covered on one side with zinc. This serves to trim lamps upon in the morning, and any kerosene that may drop upon it helps to keep it clean, instead of soiling it as it would the table. Once a week it should be scoured off with kerosene and ashes or brick dust and vinegar. Still another way to save table scrubbing is to have a yard of zinc nailed over one end of it. The nails used must be copper tacks.

CARE OF LAMPS.

The regular trimming of lamps is one of the necessary morning duties, and appropriately follows the bed-room work, although it can be done during any ten vacant minutes there may be before going up stairs. The dovetailing of work, to make one task fit in with another so that there are no lost minutes, is the secret of accomplishing very much in a short time. If you have no regular lamp scissors, (which cost very little, save your others, and also save the bits of carbonized wick from dropping about,) devote an old pair to the purpose.

In trimming the wick, cut off as little of the charred part as possible, generally it is sufficient just to clip off any inequality of the burned surface. Some people do not cut the wick at all, but simply wipe it off with paper, but the edge sometimes remains ragged after this; then the scissors may be used with advantage to make it even; if the flame is not even, you may be sure there is some tiny point on the wick; see that the corners are very slightly rounded off, to prevent points of flame. If they are cut off too much, however, the flame will be too narrow, and the light not so good as the size of the wick will allow.

Every drop of oil must be wiped from the burner, and nothing answers for this purpose better than newspaper which can be immediately burned. If a cloth is used, it must either be washed out immediately, or it will cause the place in which it is kept, and everything near it, to smell of kerosene.

When you are sure the lamp and burner are quite free from oil, polish the chimney. The common bulbous chimney is best cleaned, when only dim, with soft newspaper; if smoked and fly spotted, wash it in soapy hot water, rinse it in clear *hot* water, and wipe it dry. Do not be satisfied to place a chimney that is not brightly polished on a lamp ; like a well black-ened stove, a clean lamp gives an air of cleanliness and cheerfulness to the plainest room, while a hand-some one in which the odor of kerosene is percepti-ble, and a smoke dimmed chimney visible, will seem neglected and depressing.

For the cylinder chimney which is the most diffi-cult to clean, I have found nothing so good, after trying all sorts of contrivances, as the brush with wire handle sold for the purpose. With daily use of this, the chimney seldom needs washing and is always bright. The brush must be used *dry;* hold the chim-ney in your left hand with a duster or newspaper to prevent your touch from dimming it, then with the right hand push the brush sharply up and down, pol-ish the outside with paper; less than a minute's work each day will keep the chimney in perfect order.

Once in a while wash the brush and dry it thoroughly.

The burners of all lamps require washing in soap and hot water once a week.

When lamps cease to give a good light, many people throw them away and get new. There is usually nothing the matter, except that the perforations are choked with carbon and dust. Boil them for half an hour, in an old saucepan in which you have a good teaspoonful of washing soda to each quart of water; rinse them and set them to dry. This will generally remedy the difficulty.

CHAPTER VII.

WEDNESDAY is the day which most house-keepers feel to be the one of comparative leisure. That day may conveniently be reserved for extra duties. In the fall the bulk of the canning or pickling or preserving each week, may be done on that day. Occasionally it happens that fruit must be used, and then the housekeeper must do it without regard to days, but when she has the matter within her control, Wednesday interferes with her general work less.

At this season the preserving is over, although for those whose absence from home, sickness, or other cause prevented them making a sufficient supply from summer and fall fruits, there still remains orange marmalade, apple jelly, and a very useful French marmalade called *raisine*, excellent for children. On certain fall and winter Wednesdays, too, the careful housekeeper may choose to utilize what would otherwise be thrown away: orange and lemon peels. A few jars of candied peels, are invaluable through the winter. They make a plain cake into something that is superior; the same with ginger-bread or cookies, and there is no such fragrant addition to mincemeat as these peels, and they take the place of citron for many purposes.

Although, as I have said, recipes for cooking will be the rare exception in these papers, when one occurs to me that I think may not be found in the usual cookery books, I will give it. Candying peels comes under this head, I think, I therefore give directions how to do them.

Keep two jars or crocks half full of strong salt and water. Into one drop any orange peels you may have; into the other lemon peels. The thicker the peels the better for the purpose. Those from Havana oranges are not suitable. If they have been squeezed, rid them of the skin and pulp, but do not touch the white. Oranges that have been used for the table, if the peels have been neatly divided in halves or quarters, and not soiled by children, may be used for this purpose. If many lemons are not used in the house, it will pay to take advantage of their cheap season, when a quarter of a hundred may be bought for a small sum. The juice may be boiled into syrup and bottled, and the peels serve for candying. The peels will keep in salt and water, in a cool place, for months, provided the brine always covers them; or they may be only left a week in it.

TO CANDY LEMON PEELS.

Boil the peels until very tender, but not at all broken, changing the water till it no longer tastes salt. They generally take from two to three hours to become tender. Strain the water from them when you are sure they are done. Lemon peels have the peculiarity of hardening in syrup, unless they are quite tender when put in it.

You can candy the peels in large pieces like citron which is really the proper way, although it may be convenient sometimes to have them ready for use. If you decide to candy them in large pieces, lay the peels in a preserving kettle; pour over them as many pints of water as will just cover them; add a pound of granulated sugar to each pint; let it boil up, then put the kettle where the peels will simmer till they *are clear;* you may then let the syrup boil fast till there is very little left. They require watching at this stage, for they will easily burn. You may lift each piece out and lay it on a dish on which granulated sugar has been sprinkled, and, covering them thickly with sugar, put them in a cool oven till dry; or you may do what is after all less trouble, and produces much handsomer results. This is after they have boiled till clear in the syrup, to lay each piece on an oiled dish; let them get cool while you boil a pound or two of sugar (according to the number of peels you have) with a gill of water to the pound, till it "hairs," then dip each piece of peel into the candy and lay it on an oiled dish to dry.

If you prefer convenience to effect, you can cut the peels, when they are boiled tender, into chips, ready for use. To do this, cut them into strips an inch wide; pile three or four, one on the other, and cut into little thin strips about as wide as a match.

Make a syrup of a pound of sugar to each pint of

water; throw in the chips. Boil them slowly till clear, then faster till nearly all moisture has evaporated, then stir in a cupful more of sugar and put them where they can get dry, but cannot burn. When there is no longer any moisture, spread them thinly on sieves and put them in a cool oven or over the register to dry. If you have no sieves, spread them on tins thickly sprinkled with sugar, and stir them up from time to time. When cold pack away in glass jars for use.

When the peels are cut small it is better not to candy too many in one kettle, as they are apt to dry in masses instead of separate.

Orange peels are candied just in the same way but do not take quite so long to boil. Never put both lemon and orange peel in the same salt water, nor candy them together.

Raisinè also is a preserve less well known than it deserves to be; I therefore give a recipe for that also:

RAISINÈ.

Take a dozen fine, large apples. Peel and quarter them, put them over a slow fire with a cupful of California sherry, or the same quantity of cider and a pound of sugar. When they have stewed tender, stone five pounds of fine, pulpy Valencia raisins, with enough water to prevent them burning; leave them to cook very slowly until they appear dissolved, and the whole is stiff. Beat the whole through a colander and then through a sieve, unless you have one of the squeezing machines which work on the principle of a lemon squeezer, and save much labor in making marmalade, jellies, etc.   Pack away in small jars and when about to use, cut it in thin slices and dust each with confectioner's sugar.   This is delicious eaten with cream.

Orange marmalade is probably too well known to require a recipe; but before quitting the subject of preserves I wish to suggest a plan which, from my own experience, saves much time and vexation.

A NEW WAY TO COVER JELLY.

I allude to the covering of jams and jellies.   The trouble of papering them securely is, to many, the worst part of making them, especially when it is necessary to make a large quantity.   Much time may be saved by using waxed paper, which can be bought at the confectioners' supply stores, very cheaply. Twelve cents' worth will be sufficient for a whole season.   Cut a round of the paper to fit the top of your jelly glass, and have a quarter of an inch or so margin; lay the waxed paper on the jelly, press it with your fingers gently till there are no air bubbles under it, then press the margin closely round the inside of the glass.   This is all you need to do; jelly so put up will rarely have mildew on it, and keep in every way better than with the usual brandied paper and second paper cover.

MENDING.

I have spoken of Wednesday being usually the most convenient for mending, and even in families where it takes more than one day, that may be the best on which to begin it, when other things do not prevent.

It is a good plan to have a small basket near the ironing board while ironing, and as the articles needing repair are ironed, lay them in it. In this way the tiny split in a napkin or towel, which will not take five minutes to darn, will not be unnoticed until it has assumed too large proportions for it to escape.

In mending, "a stitch in time" does indeed "save nine,"—or ninety-nine. The stocking with tiny hole and thin spot which can be so neatly darned (the thin spot closely run on the wrong side with a stitch bearly visible on the right) this week, as to be hardly perceptible, will, if left for another wearing, have a large hole which necessitates a large, unsightly darn that will be three times the work.

In darning children's colored stockings, be sure the cotton is of good quality and will not fade, or else, darn you never so neatly, after one wash the stocking will be shabby, by reason of the faded darns. At any first rate store darning cotton, warranted fast dyes, are sold, and may be relied upon.

Table linen should be darned with very fine linen floss or, better still, the raveling from a strip of damask.

Window shades, chintz or any starched article that is not often washed, can be neatly repaired while being ironed by laying over the spot a small piece of material matching in texture. This of course must be starched and wet; the iron will paste them together. Chinese laundrymen turn this kind of mending to account with bachelors' shirts and collars.

PROGRAMME OF WORK.

WEDNESDAY.

After the regular work has been got through with, what extra work is to be done on Wednesday must depend on the circumstances of the family.

Preserving, mending, bread making, window cleaning (if there are too many windows, or too much sweeping, for them to be done on sweeping day) may all be conveniently done on the one " off " day of the week.

It is a good plan to wash lamp burners on this day (see full directions chapter V), as it saves time from those more crowded with work. Nevertheless it is well to let the busy days carry their own burden, so as to keep Wednesday as far as possible for the unusual work, and if none presents itself, for a little of the play that would agree with our constitution so well if we could try it oftener.

CHAPTER VIII.

IN a small house the sweeping can often be done in one day, and Friday is set apart for it, but it makes housekeeping easy, so to divide work that no one day shall be over full of it. It can then be performed easily, and so thoroughly that " house-cleaning " will not be the time of terror it so often is. I therefore recommend sweeping the upper rooms on Thursday and leaving the lower till Friday. It is not always necessary to thoroughly sweep the spare rooms every week; they should be gone over with the sweeper and nicely dusted. Every other week the carpet broom may be used; this is a question, however, which every housekeeper must decide for herself. I wish to remind her that there is no merit in doing needless work.

· If you have pretty knicknacks round the room, dust them and lay them on the bed, draw up shades as far as they will go, pin up curtains, and for very delicate ones, it is nice when you have folded and pinned them quite short to slip over each an old pillow case and pin it as near the curtain pole as you can.

Cover the bed and anything likely to get dusty with old sheets. For carpeted rooms there is nothing better to sweep with than damp tea leaves, but they are apt to stain matting, for sweeping which, a newspaper, dipped in water till very soft and wrung out, then torn into shreds and flung round the floor, is excellent. The flue and bed-room dust is so light that, without something to gather it, it is apt, with the most careful sweeping, to float in the air when disturbed, rather than remain in front of the broom.

If there is a fire in the room, remove the ashes before beginning to sweep, brushing them gently from the stove wherever they may have lodged, and if the stove is a very warm one, and you leave it dormant the better part of the time, take this opportunity to remove clinkers and give it a thorough raking, as, if you leave it to do till a day or two later, your room will be full of dust again.

Leave the stove to be blackened after the sweeping is done.

Sweep with a long, steady stroke, taking care to form a habit of raising the broom at the end of the stroke in such a way as to prevent dust raising. Watch some women sweep, and you will understand what I mean. They will work hard, and sweep as if they were digging; a small cloud of dust will follow the end of the broom every time it is raised.

Be careful to go into every corner with the end of your broom, and to brush all dust from between carpet or matting and skirting board, as here is where moths love to harbor. Sweep from all sides of the room to the center. This sweeping to center instead of the door may strike some readers as an innovation, but if they will consider a moment they will see that there is no reason whatever for dragging the dust all over the room. Sweeping toward the *center* of a sixteen feet square room, you only sweep the dust eight feet each way, instead of carrying it before the broom the whole sixteen feet. Short, quick strokes of the broom are apt to scatter the dust, especially when the stroke ends with an upward jerk, as I have often seen it do, when the broom is in the hands of vigorous girls who imagine they are getting over the ground much more rapidly by hurried movements than they would if they took greater pains. But hurry is not speed; some women are quick and thorough, others slow and thorough, but the one always hurrying, is rarely either quick or thorough, she makes work all the time she is doing it.

Before beginning to sweep, open such windows as will not interfere with the dust; I mean such as will not blow it about. Often people throw open every window and sweep, in a sort of small whirlwind. Dust cannot go out through a window against which the wind is blowing, therefore such a window is to be kept carefully shut, unless there is one opposite. When the sweeping is done and the dust all carefully gathered into a dustpan, then open all windows if you choose, so that a thorough draught may carry out the particles in the air. The room can now be left for dust to settle while you go to another.

For the rooms needing less thorough sweeping, use the sweeper, but before doing so, go round the skirting board and in the corners with the broom, brushing out the dust. To many this will seem as much

trouble as sweeping the room, but it is far from being
so, because the preparation and dusting will be so
much less.

When the dust has well settled, tie a duster over
your broom and sweep the walls and ceiling, dust the
tops of furniture, doors and skirting board. Wash
all porcelain on the washstand and the marble, or if
you use a toilette cloth, change it. Rub the looking
glass with a dry duster; if spotted, use a damp cloth
first. If you are particular to have the dark polish
so much admired on mirrors, keep some washing blue
in powder tied in muslin enclosed in a box, and when
polishing mirrors dab the muslin gently over the
glass; enough blue will come through, then polish,
taking care to remove any blue powder from the
frame, etc.

Dust the sashes of the windows and clean the windows. In winter it is not always possible to clean
windows when they need it, but make a rule on sweeping day to go all over the panes with a dry duster.
This will often be all that is necessary for weeks, as
it removes all the smoke and dust, and while the snow
lies the outside does not get dirty, the soil is all inside.
Do not in frosty weather, attempt to wet the glass.
If the windows are much soiled you can wet a sponge
with alcohol and go over them.

When cleaning windows do not use soap; a very
little soda, borax, or ammonia, in the water, will be
best, but water alone will do. Use a sponge or cloth,
wrung almost dry. Go over the entire window with
this, taking care to go into every corner with your

forefinger or the handle of an old tooth brush covered with the damp cloth.

When you have done the last pane, go over them quickly with a soft, dry duster, beginning with the pane you first wetted. If you work briskly it is a very few minutes work to clean a window.

Polish off with an old newspaper, and do not be satisfied until you have removed every blur.

When the rooms are all in order and the doors closed, proceed to the corridors, and bath-room if there is one ; this will probably have oilcloth on the floor unless it is of hard wood, the cleaning of which will be spoken of later. Oilcloth, however, needs only wiping with warm water and flannel wrung half dry and rinsed till it comes from the floor clean, showing that it has taken up the dirt, then wipe with a coarse cloth. This will preserve oil cloth bright double the time it usually keeps so. Free use of water, which gets under it and cannot dry away, rots it, while scrubbing with soap destroys the color in a short time.

Scour out the bath tub with soap and fine sand if it is not enameled. Rub up the faucets, and every few weeks rub the wood work of the bath with furniture oil; this will preserve it and prevent the shabby look it so soon gets. If the bath is painted inside, simply go over it with a flannel dipped in whitening.

However good your plumbing may be, your security will be greater if, every week, you use a disinfectant liberally. One that costs very little, and is perfectly odorless, is made by dissolving a heaped teaspoonful of nitrate of lead in a quart of boiling water. Stir with a stick and then add it to a pail of cold water. This is odorless and will not stain; it costs about three cents, and if it is thrown once a week down the bath-tub closet and stationary wash bowl, it will be money well spent. Another disinfectant may be preferred, only use something of the kind *regularly* on a certain day. If the day for doing a thing is fixed, it generally gets done; if "once a week," means any day, it is often forgotten. This is the reason why, although I am not an advocate for cast iron rules of housekeeping, and should not make a trouble of it, if circumstances made it necessary, or even pleasant, for the whole order of work to be so changed for a week or two that nothing was done on its appointed day and some things not done at all, yet it no doubt saves nerves and time to have regular rules and days. In these papers I hope it will be clearly understood that I am only making suggestions, not laying down laws; one can only do that for individual cases, and what suits my house and circumstances, or those of some of my readers, cannot possibly suit all. I hope only that the inexperienced housekeeper may be able to form for herself some weekly plan of work from what I write.

Silver cleaning is a convenient Thursday task. It is well to keep about the number of silver articles required for daily use separate from the full number you keep out; for instance, although you may only be four in a family, you will probably have a dozen spoons and forks in the basket, but if you keep part aside and use the others, except when you need the whole for changes, you will be sure of having two or three perfectly bright for visitors without going to your locked silver. Those only once or twice used, too, will not need the weekly cleaning. This may seem a small matter to save, but to women without a servant every minute saved is so much gain ; others more fortunate can ignore these small matters.

I speak of a weekly cleaning, but, as a matter of fact, if the silver is washed as I have recommended, it will be almost as bright at the week's end as at the beginning. It is the washing in lukewarm water and drying when cold, that gives the dull, leaden appearance after a few days' use. Silver dried out of hot water on a clean cloth, will really be always bright, and thorough cleaning once in a month will suffice, only requiring each piece to be rubbed with a dry leather each week. But unless you do the washing of it with your own hands, the probabilities are that it will require the weekly cleaning.

There are several approved ways of cleaning silver, all good, and I give them that you may take the way you prefer.

You require a small sponge or piece of flannel, a soft chamois skin, a clean dry duster, and a silver brush. If you have no chamois, keep old, undressed kid gloves for the purpose.

Rub all articles that are badly stained. such as egg spoons, etc., with salt; it will remove stains more easily than anything else. The simplest way, and one of the best, is to mix a little whitening in a saucer with water enough to make a thick paste, to this add a few drops of household ammonia.

Instead of the ammonia and water, you may moisten the whitening with alcohol, or with simple water; whichever you use, the process is the same.

Many prefer to use the articles sold ready prepared for cleaning silver; several are very good, but do not be tempted into trying any new article, warranted to give extraordinary brilliance without labor, buy only those that have stood the test of time.

CHAPTER IX.

THE WASTE OF THE HOUSEHOLD — TO CLARIFY FAT — TO MAKE SOFT SOAP WITHOUT BOILING.

I HAVE been trying to find space to say something about the waste of a household, but other matters have crowded it out. It would astonish the heads of some families who believe themselves fairly economical, to know how far economy may be carried in a household forced to it. However, I am not supposing extreme cases, and will only speak of a few points on which money might be saved. A great deal of coal is lost by some people who think it does not pay to sift ashes. From the furnace, perhaps not, especially if you have to hire a man to do it, but in a small house where the work is not very heavy, the cinders from the kitchen are so well worth doing that a scuttle nearly full of good fuel will result from the morning sifting; if the sifter is fixed on a barrel and covered, it is not disagreeable work, nor will it take ten minutes to sift cinders from two or three fires.

Another source of waste is the fat. In some houses everything is put away for soap fat, which is sold to the junk man for a trifle, and lard bought for cooking; in others, beef fat is kept and all else thrown away. As a matter of fact, most families would have little need to buy lard, and soap only for laundry purposes, if all fat were saved.

It is needless to say, perhaps, that the fat of beef is as wholesome as butter, or that hog's lard is one of the most unwholesome ingredients of our food, yet, in spite of this acknowledged fact, it is the beef fat that is often thrown away and lard that is purchased for use. There are two reasons for this, no doubt. The lard comes ready rendered and in neat shape, and although it is high in price and largely adulterated (even when nothing is added to it, *it is said* that what we buy as lard from the grocer has had lard oil already made from it), it is bought for convenience. The second reason may be that, although it is known beef fat is wholesome, it is not known so widely, that every bit of dripping, every bit of fat steak, the skimming from water in which beef has boiled, can be tried out and clarified into the purest and sweetest beef lard.

Have a crock into which you put all your scraps of clean fat pork, veal or beef, all fat but mutton, every day, and once a week bring them to the kitchen, cut them small, and put them in a saucepan with a small cup of water to prevent burning. Leave them at the back of the stove while you are doing other things, and when the bits have all shrunken to nothing and look crisp it is done; strain off into a bowl. If only scraps of fresh fat were in the crock you need only turn it out of the bowl in a cake when cold, scrape off the bottom in case of sediment and put it away. If the crock also contained drippings and skimmings (it is better to have these, however, in a separate vessel), it will need clarifying; this is done by putting the cake of fat you now have, in a saucepan with a pint of boiling water and let them boil together without a cover for an hour; this will remove the taste of vegetables or anything that might otherwise taint the dripping. Throw in a teaspoonful of salt and let it get cold in a cake. Turn it out and scrape the bottom. It will now be sweet, and clear of all impurity. This should be used for frying and greasing pans.

For pastry, buy from your butcher six to ten pounds of beef fat, which, although, since the days of oleomargarine, is not such a drug in the market as before, can still be readily bought from six cents to seven cents per pound. You do not want *suet*, but the inside fat or any other. Try this out exactly as you would hog's lard. You will find that the refuse will not weigh half a pound. This wholesome beef lard, firm as butter, will go much farther than the ordinary lard you buy and cost at least three cents a pound less. This can be used in cake, biscuit, pastry, everything in fact, for which you would use lard.

In very cold weather, if there is admixture of suet, you may find beef lard too firm to rub into flour; if this prove so, try out with it one-third pork fat.

It is a great improvement, either to beef or hog's lard, to beat it with a wooden spoon till cold. Begin to beat when it is cool enough to thicken and continue till it is too stiff. It will be much whiter and finer in texture than if allowed to cool without beating.

Another much written about source of waste is the throwing away of bones, and because it is so important a part of domestic economy, I add my word to the many already spoken as to this branch of kitchen management. I know some housekeepers think unless they have large joints and many bones, it is more trouble than saving.

One lady said to me, "You always talk about boiling down bones, but how can one have bones to boil? We have chops and steaks and sometimes a small roast of beef, or a chicken, none of which make anything worth stewing down, then bones are such unmanageable things; you have to put a leg of lamb bone or a single beef rib bone into a large saucepan with quarts of water to cover it, or else the greater part sticks out, and, of course, does no good to the water."

Certainly not, but you can break the bones up, a small machine comes for the purpose, but as few bones are harder than a hickory nut, you can generally manage to crack them by laying them on a four-pound weight and giving them a blow with a hammer. *All* bones that have not been handled are good to make stock, and bruise even small ones; the smaller you can break them the better.

Of course, in a small family, you need not boil the bones each day. If they are not likely to keep, put them in the oven and bake them well, they will then keep until you have more.

A very good soup may be made of bones alone. You will find the stock, when cold, a firm jelly, but it will need to be a vegetable soup, or one flavored with them and thickened with peas or beans. But if to this stock you add a pound of chopped leg of beef to each two or three quarts, with the usual flavoring, you will have a rich, strong soup for any purpose except clear *bouillon*.

In boiling bones for stock the goodness may be considered extracted when they look quite dry and white. Scraps, fag ends of mutton chops or steak, all help, and, however fat, remember you are killing two birds with one stone, for the fat will form on the top when cold and can be taken off and clarified.

If, instead of using this bone stock for soup, you use it for hash or warming over meat for a week, you will never again be without for the purpose. Cold meat warmed simply with water and onion and flour, *if* carefully done, may be quite palatable, yet no one would say for a moment, it equalled fresh cooked meat; but if, instead of the water, gravy or stock is used you will find it as rich as any fresh meat, and it is equally nourishing, because the gravy supplies what was drawn out of the meat. So true is this, that where there could be no bone stock, it would be an economy to buy, once a week, a soup bone simply to make gravy for warming over purposes. Three pints of strong stock would cost at most twenty cents, and there would be an end of insipid dishes, by boiling it over for ten minutes, after the third day it will keep another three days in a cold place.

I have spoken of using mutton fat for soap. It should be tried out while fresh, that no disagreeable

odor may be in the house, and kept apart for the purpose.   I speak of making it into soft soap because,
unless you have more fat than you can use for that purpose, it is easier to make than hard soap, which must
be boiled, and for some hours, at least, the odors it
gives forth are not those of Araby the blest.   With
soft soap, made according to the recipe I append,
there need be no boiling, no odor.

Dissolve three pounds of potash in three quarts of
water.   Put the potash, in the lump, in an old saucepan, pour the boiling water on it, set it on the stove
and leave it till it is dissolved; it may take several
hours.   Stir it about with a stick now and then, taking care not to splash it on you, three pounds of clean
fat in a tub or small barrel.   When the potash is dissolved pour on the fat, stir well with the stick and
leave it.   Next day pour a kettle (holding at least a
gallon) of boiling water, slowly, to the potash and
fat, stirring thoroughly.   Do this every morning till
the soap is made, which you will know by it beginning to look like stiff jelly when cold, and losing all
appearance of grease, then try it; if it seems too
strong, or makes the hands rough, add more boiling
water.   The soap will be ready to use in about nine
days after it is started.

This soap is good for scrubbing, dish washing, paint
cleaning, and washing coarse cloths.

In another paper I shall have something to say of
certain much neglected means of economy, which
would not diminish but increase household comfort
and even luxury, paradoxical as this may sound.

PROGRAMME OF WORK.

BED-ROOM SWEEPING.

Dust ornaments, cover them, cover up furniture, roll up curtains and pin them. Take up ashes if there is a fire in the room, laying down a paper in front of the stove while you do it.

Then scatter tea leaves or moistened newspaper, torn in shreds, all round the room, open the windows on the opposite side from the wind, then begin to sweep, taking care to brush the corners first.

Sweep to the center of the room, gather up the dirt on a dustpan, and then throw open any other windows that will create a current of air to carry out dust; proceed to the other rooms till all are swept. Black the stoves, if there are any, then dust the rooms, beginning with walls and ceiling, which go over with the broom covered with a duster.

Wash all toilet articles, clean windows, wash any finger marks from paint. As you finish each room, look round to see that you have left nothing undone, and that no brush, cloth, or duster, remains behind you, then close the door, so that in sweeping hall or corridor and stairs the dust does not enter.

Having swept corridors and stairs and dusted the walls, windows and sashes, take a pail and warm water, wring a cloth from it and wipe along the skirting board and side of the stairs. Rinse your cloth very often, so that your work may not look smeary, because you cannot use water freely if there is carpet or matting; all you want is to remove dust more effectually than a broom will do it.

If there is a bath-room, scour out the bath with soap and sand, oil the wood work and wipe the oil-cloth with warm water and a flannel without soap.

Rub all faucets and any brass or nickel there may be.

Sweep corridor and stairs, dust bannisters and skirting board, and go over the latter and sides of the stairs with a cloth wrung out of soapy warm water.

Clean silver, taking care that it is all nicely washed in hot water.

Rub over it the following mixture:

TO CLEAN SILVER.

Whitening made into cream with diluted ammonia, or alcohol, or water, rub all dark or stained pieces well. When each is covered with a thin milky coat, leave it to dry while you go on with the rest.

When all are dry, rub off the whitening, and then polish with a leather; lastly, rub all vigorously with a brush, to remove all the cleaning material from crevices. The brush also cleans and polishes the chasing where the leather is useless.

CHAPTER X.

ON Friday, if possible, it is well to finish the work of the house, leaving Saturday for the cleansing of the kitchen, pantries, cellars, and whatever offices may be attached to it. On Saturday, too, most housekeepers make cake, cookies, pies, etc., for the week, although in families where pastry is required in small quantity, but very good, puff or half puff paste is better made on Friday, to be used on Saturday. The larder, safe, or refrigerator should, of course, be inspected *every* morning, and in *cold* weather it may be found better each morning to lay on one plate pieces of fat to be tried out, on another fag ends of beefsteak, of chops, bones, etc., and make Friday the day for disposing of them, so that on Saturday you begin afresh. Possibly each day the left over meat may be too little to make any dish, but never was any maxim more worthy of the housekeepers's recollection than the good old Scotch one, " Mony a mickle makes a muckle." One fag end of steak may not seem worth making into hash (although a small sweet or white potato, and the end of even *one* steak will make hash for one person's breakfast), but three or four will make as nice a stew or hash for three or four people as if you were to buy meat expressly, and you save exactly the price of meat for one meal. Or, if you are not in need yourself, and charitably give away your broken food, you will do infinitely more good by giving one good meal to a family of children than allowing bits of cold meat to be given each day.

Beggars will always be beggars, and I cannot say I advise giving relief to that class, but there is many a hard-working woman and her children insufficiently nourished whom a hot meat supper once a week may go far to keep in health, and cost nothing but the little trouble.

However, this is a digression, on a subject which requires more thought than could be given in a mere aside—I mean the subject of charity, when and how it is wise to give—one thing only I will say, if you give, be sure it is where it will aid the self-helping and not foster pauperism, and then give in the shape that will do most good, even if it takes some trouble.

To "return to our muttons," or, in this case, steaks, there may be among your fag ends less of steak than anything else—a single chop, a bit of veal, half a slice, or less, of boiled ham; never mind, so much the better for stew. The ends of steak are often considered quite useless. An excellent housekeeper once said to me, "I can use every scrap in my house except the end of beefsteak; that is sheer waste, for we always have steak broiled, and the blackish smoke makes it unfit for any use when cold."

I could have made two answers: (1.) There was no real necessity for it to be black; (2.) that if it be black, a bath of boiling water would remove it. But the lady was making a statement, not asking advice, so I refrained from saying what I say now,—cold meat, that has unfortunately been blackened in broiling, should be put into a colander, set in a bowl, and boiling water be poured over it. Stir it about quickly to rinse well, then lift the colander and drain. This disposes of the black grease, if it is there.

Now, I suppose, although it is somewhat aside from my purpose, I had better tell how to make a few right good dishes of these oft despised remains. You must remember, from cold roast meat you will not have nearly so good material for warming over as from these pieces of steak, because they are so much less cooked the first time. There is usually a thick band of fat to the end of steak; trim that nearly all away and lay it aside. Your meat is now ready to make either of the following stews:

STEWED BEEF.

Cut the beef into inch square pieces; flour each; cut a small carrot, a small turnip, and a large onion into slices, put the fat you trimmed off into a deep spider or a saucepan, let it get very hot, lay in the vegetables, cover, and leave them to brown (not burn,) stirring occasionally. When they are all nicely browned, pour on them a pint of boiling water, and lay in the meat; put with it a moderate teaspoonful of salt, half a saltspoonful of pepper, with two or three coarse stalks of celery, if you have them, cut fine. Let all stew very gently for two hours at least, or until the meat is quite tender, but remember, if it has *boiled* or stewed fast, it will never be that, nor would it, if you made your stew of tenderloin.   Skim free from fat and serve.

ROPA VIEGA STEW.

Cut the beef into small pieces.   Cut the fat into a spider; slice into it three large onions; let them fry brown.   Dredge each piece of meat with flour, pepper and salt, using a small teaspoonful of the first and a quarter one of pepper.   Add the meat and half a *small* can of tomatoes, or six fresh ones, sliced, to the onions; let all stew two hours very slowly and closely covered.   Use no water unless the stew is quite too thick, when add a little boiling water.

These sound as if they took more time to prepare than they really do.   You will understand that the vegetables in the first recipe can be put on quite early, and once they have gone into the very hot pan, can after the first few minutes be drawn to the back of the stove, while you or your maid go about other tasks; remember only to give an occasional stir to them when you are near the range.   After the meat and tomatoes are added, you need to watch it perhaps for another five minutes to discover just on which part of the range it will cook slowly enough.   You will, after that, look at it once or twice to see that the simmer has not ceased altogether, nor yet become too fast.

Another dish that may be conveniently made of cold mutton, veal, pork, beef, or a bit of all—any odds and ends, in fact—and if you have also cold calf's liver, so much the better ; if not. get a *lamb's* liver. This is a dish for an epicure, although the materials may seem only fit to make into an everyday hash.

MOCK TERRAPIN.

Cut the meat into dice; do not chop it, but cut it as small as green peas. If you use fresh liver, wash and trim it and set it in a hot oven for half an hour. Keep the gravy from it, cut it up in slices half an inch thick, then across and across into small dice. Shake over the meat and liver a small tablespoonful of flour, a teaspoonful of made mustard, as much cayenne as will go on half a silver dime, the same of ground cloves or three whole cloves; stir all together, put into a stewpan with the gravy from the liver, and a small teacupful of boiling water, with which rinse the pan in which the liver was baked. Keep this *well covered* on a part of the range where it will keep boiling hot but not boil. Just before serving, chop two hard boiled eggs rather fine ; add them with a lump of butter the size of an egg and a wine glass of wine or good cider. Serve with a cut lemon.

Now, only the last of these three dishes need cost more than ordinary hash; the addition of the vegetables, costing a few cents, so increases the quantity of food that one need not count their cost, and I invite you to see how much better a meal of one will seem than one of hash. I said I hoped once in a while to be useful to those who cater for boarders. Will not this last dish seem a sumptuous change to those who grumble at too frequent hash ?

Now we return again to the larder and its refuse. If there are chop bones, steak bones, the carcass of a turkey or fowl well denuded of meat, crack them all up with a hatchet as small as you can; set them on with a teaspoonful of salt and two quarts of water, let them boil all day slowly; by night there will be from a pint to a quart (according to the number of bones) of broth, which will jelly when cold, and will do for gravy or to warm over meat in during the week.

If you have skimmings from stews or soup, odd pieces of fat left from roasts, trimmings of chops, etc., cut all into small pieces and put them into a saucepan with a little water to "try out." When the water has boiled away, the bits of meat and fat will be crisp. Skim these out of the fat, put a little salt and a pint of boiling water to the fat, and boil fast ten minutes; pour into a bowl and set it away. Next day take the cake of fat from the water, scrape every bit of sediment and water from the bottom, and this fat will be good for any kind of frying. If these cakes accumulate, melt them all down together in a lard pail. (See also Chapter IX., "Wastes of the Household.")

If the cheese is reduced to a small crusty piece which you do not care to put on the table, and may be quite sure Delia will not eat, have it grated up; an ounce will make a little glass dishful for the table; if you have more than this or do not want it there, put in a glass bottle ready for macaroni, etc.

The bread box needs scalding and drying once a week, in summer twice. If there is no sun in which to stand it, put it for a few minutes on a part of your range where it will dry thoroughly.

All pieces of bread may either be made into a pudding or dried for use, many people dry crust and crumb together. This is a mistake, as the crumb is spoilt for many uses if there is the least admixture of crust. Cut crust from the crumb, put both into separate pans in a very cool oven, be careful the crumb does not color. When it has quite dried out and is crisp, roll it fine and put it away to use for queen pudding, frying, turkey dressing, or the many uses to which fine bread crumbs are put. Bake the crusts till perfectly brown and crisp, roll them, taking care to remove any pieces that may be very dark in color. When they are quite fine, put them away for use. Brown sifted crumbs are useful for sprinkling over boiled ham. They ornament many dishes not otherwise brown enough—such as macaroni—and if cake tins, after being greased, are strewn with them and the superfluous ones shaken out, the cake will be much handsomer. Glass fruit jars, too defective to use for canning, are excellent receptacles for crumbs, etc.

I have indicated these things for Friday's special work, not because they might not as well be done any other day, just whenever the time presents itself, but because, unless you are very severe with yourself, what has no special time for the doing is apt to be neglected or forgotten, while, if you have a certain hour on a certain day for the task, it will be done if you have a moderate regard for system.

CHAPTER XI.

IN small houses the whole of the sweeping may be done on Friday, although, as it is always well to avoid a heavy day's work when two moderate ones can as easily be managed, as I have recommended in last instalment, bedroom sweeping and the cleaning of bedroom windows may be apportioned to Thursday. In large houses, if the sweeping is to be done by one person, such division is absolutely necessary.

Before sweeping dining-room, parlor, library, etc., roll up the curtains, portieres, etc., and slip old pillow cases over them. Brush the lounges, going well into every corner with a brush kept for the purpose. If you are unfortunate enough to have tufted furniture, this brushing must be very thorough, in order to prevent moths and also the packets of dust that will lodge in the plaits round the buttons. No mere surface brushing will do this; every fold and button must have attention if you would preserve the beauty of the covering, and sad to say, the better the quality and stuffing of tufted furniture the more difficult the care of it is. Once the dust has been allowed to accumulate round the buttons, it is almost an impossible task ever to get it completely free, although hours of work, patience, and an old toothbrush will do much. Brushes come expressly for tufted furniture, but although they may help to keep new furniture clean, they are but little use in removing dust once it has become impacted in the crevices by neglect.

Lounges are usually too large to put outside, but chairs are better brushed out of doors, if you have convenience for it. In cities this, of course, is often impossible, but they are the better for the airing where it can be done, otherwise brush them and set them in another room. Cover the larger pieces of furniture with old sheets or any available covers. Remove small articles of *bric-a-brac* from the walls, dust them, lay them on a table, and cover it. Plush frames, hangings, etc., should also be taken down or covered. Ornamental plants should be removed, or, if too large, the leaves carefully dusted and covered, as nothing so soon destroys the beauty of plants as dust—it chokes and blights them.

When all superfluous articles are removed, begin to clean the room by taking up ashes. On sweeping day do not let the fire draw until the grate is thoroughly blacked and polished. If there are nickel trimmings, polish with kerosene and whitening, or with plate powder. If the trimmings are of bright steel, fine emery powder should be used. By far the most general fashion at present, however, is brass, both for fire irons and grates. This is far more easily cleaned than polished steel, and, if never allowed to get much tarnished, is really very easy to keep bright. Brass in good condition and cleaned weekly requires only rubbing with a little whitening and a leather; discolored and neglected brass requires hard work the first time it is cleaned, and the use of one or other of the preparations I give in the programme of work.

There are many diverse opinions about carpet sweeping. Some good housekeepers maintain that to throw any damp substance on the floor to prevent dust rising is a mistake, also that every window should be open and the dust allowed to rise and be blown out—the more wind the better. Others, whose authority appears to me equally good, say, and I agree with them, that to sweep in a gale with nothing to "lay the dust" is to make a dirty, suffocating business of one that is otherwise not unpleasant. The fact seems to me that the dust so raised will only be blown out so far as it lies in the course of the wind, the rest will lodge on the walls and every part that may intercept it; and unless there is a window directly opposite the one from which the wind comes, there can be no blowing of the dust *out* at all; it will not go out against the wind, it will rather be blown back.

As to the idea that you need to raise the dust from the carpet, that is quite true; you want the dust out of the carpet, but you do not want it to fly all over the place. Those who object to using wet paper or tea leaves to lessen the dust must be under the impression that they in some way prevent the dust from leaving the carpet, and that they simply roll over the surface of the carpet. The fact is, if you sweep with a long, light stroke, the damp leaves will prevent the flue and dust from rising by taking it to themselves.

I have mentioned only damp tea leaves, and moistened paper where the leaves might stain, because I prefer these myself, but others are in favor of flinging wet bran over the carpet, others again prefer salt. I will only give a word of caution as to the use of salt. If your room is not very sunny and dry, you may have the unpleasant experience of a friend of mine who, after a long course of weekly sweeping with salt, began to find on certain days a very unpleasant smell in her parlor. In winter it had not been perceptible, but as the spring days came, every damp one her parlor took on the disagreeable odor of a shut up "best room," and this one was never shut up. It was a puzzle to herself and friends, no one could account for it, the whole house was airy and dry; the only remedy seemed to be a fire,—a few hours of hot fire would remove it, but only for a time. At last, just before the May cleaning, the lady put her hand one damp day on the carpet; when she lifted it, it was wet. She examined the carpet, and found it covered with a fine dew! Thus the odor was accounted for; every damp day the salt that remained in the carpet, although quite invisible, " gave."

I *know* this story to be true. Whether it would be possible by the most thorough sweeping to remove every bit of so fine a substance as salt from a Brussels carpet I will not say, but we know, by the heavy dew a very tiny sprinkling of salt on an exposed surface will cause in wet weather, that the amount required to produce dampness in a carpet would be very small. I must also say I have known carpets to be continually swept with salt with no such unpleasant results, the difference is in the room.

In all carpet sweeping great care must be taken to brush well round the skirting board. This is the favorite spot for the moths to breed. Should you suspect their existence, lay a wet cloth, folded about three inches wide, on the carpet round the skirting board, and on this press a very hot iron. The steam caused by this process will kill both moth and eggs, and there need be no fear of injuring the carpet. I have said a *wet* cloth, because I mean more than merely damp, but it must not be dripping wet. A cloth wrung out of water as dry as you can will be right.

I have, in the last number, gone into methods of sweeping, and my reason for preferring to sweep to the center of a room. In so doing I was taking for granted that the larger number of my readers will still have the old-time carpet instead of the more fashionable rug. Those who have these, unless they do away with their advantages by using "filling" or border, have one of the cares of housekeeping lessened. Large, handsome center rugs cannot easily be taken up and shaken every week, but they can be gone over thoroughly with the sweeper (and for rugs I do not think the broom is any improvement on the machine); they can then be turned some distance back towards the middle, and all dust swept from underneath.

Smaller rugs can, of course, be taken up and shaken every week. The Wilton, felt, or ingrain "fillings" often used, add to the work very much, as they show every speck, being of solid color and in a dusty street, seem to require sweeping every day to be really bright.

Wilton filling should not be swept at the same time as the rug it surrounds, which has usually some lighter colors, and the flue from these will attach itself to the darker pile. Sweep the rug first and take up the dust, then go round the room to sweep the filling or border.

If any reader is hesitating between rugs and carpets, let me advise rugs for every reason, but without the filling. By having a rug with a filling round it you have compromised between fashion, which dictates rugs, and the common deal floor, which forbids, or seems to do so, the use of stain. But rugs have more than fashion to recommend them,—they are healthy, cleanly, and economical. If you *must* cover boards, you do away with all three advantages.

Now, always supposing I am speaking to those about to make a change, is the difficulty so great? If you are going to have handsome carpets and Wilton filling, I think it will cost very little more than the filling to have a plain hardwood border laid down. What is called parquet flooring is moderate in price, and, of course, the expense only occurs once in a lifetime. To those whose means do not extend to this, and who are thinking of some lower priced border, I would still say, if your boards are only uneven, get a carpenter to smooth them; if the planks are wide apart, as, unfortunately, in low priced houses built a few years ago they often are, this same carpenter will, I think, for less by far than your filling would cost, lay in narrow slats, so that you may stain and shellac, and the result be very good. (Recipes for staining, etc., will be given in the chapter on Housecleaning.)

If your boards are gray with being for years under carpet, let me give you a hint. I was visiting, some years ago, at the house of a well known artist, at Chelsea (London), and was struck by the color of the floors of halls, stairs, and rooms. It looked a beautiful gray wood, with markings paler and darker. I was puzzled for a moment to know what kind of wood it could be, for it was not well joined and the grain was not that of a hardwood, when all at once it dawned on me,—the artist had simply utilized the coloring which time and bad scrubbing had given. The house was old—not for Chelsea; it was new by the side of Carlyle's in the next street, but at least forty or fifty years old; the floors had not the wide interstices we are too familiar with, but it had been intended for carpet, and no special care had been taken with it. Then, as they were always covered, they had not had the vigorous scrubbing that the boards meant to be visible in England are always subjected to, and the artist had done nothing to improve their defects, but had simply had them polished, probably shellacked and rubbed down once or twice, then finished, but the effect was harmonious and beautiful.

If you have hardwood floors, or the simply stained and shellacked pine, the whole beauty and freshness of the room will depend on their being kept bright and free from dust; sweeping with a *hair* broom every morning and washing once a week will secure this, except in long dry spells, or if there is much coal dust in winter, when a damp cloth must *follow* the broom when the latter is insufficient to remove the dusty appearance, but never in this or any other case allow the damp cloth to replace a broom. Too many servants think they need not sweep the floors or oilcloth if they are going to wash it; the result is a cloudy, half-cleaned look. Once in a while, every fourth week perhaps, the water used for washing stained or hardwood floors should be hot, and have a tablespoonful of turpentine and the same of oil in it, the cloth be wrung out of this and used to wipe the floors. Lightwood floors, ash, etc., are brightened by the use of skimmed milk instead of water.

After sweeping the carpet, go over the ceiling and walls with a clean duster tied over a broom, if you have not the proper holder. If you have rugs and stained floors, do this before washing them. Then clean windows, brushing the outside shutters carefully and wash the sills outside. This should always be done unless the weather is very severe, but every sweeping day without exception go over the inside of the windows with a dry duster, carefully dusting sashes and sills. A great deal of smoke from the closed house remains on windows in severe weather and dims them, but it will all come off with a dry cloth.

Mirrors should receive the same weekly attention. A small sponge dipped in alcohol quickly rubbed over the whole surface, which is then polished, is the easiest way; but the usual damp cloth and chamois is only a few minutes' work, after which daub a little powdered indigo tied up in muslin over the glass; it will add brilliancy to the surface.

The frames of pictures, tops of doors, etc., should be dusted with a feather duster, and this brings me to the question of dusting.

This should always be very thorough at least once a week, and clean soft cloths (cheese cloth makes excellent dusters) used for the purpose — not the feather duster which is very useful in its place, but is not by any means to replace a cotton duster. All tables and wooden furniture should be gone over daily with a soft cotton duster, and a slight rub accompanying the motion; so treated, furniture improves with age. This one rub daily as the duster passes over it will be an immense amount of rubbing in the course of years, and the articles will get brighter and smoother with time, and yet never have had one hour's labor bestowed; while, if the feather duster were used entirely, the highly polished furniture will get dull in a year or two and need repolishing, and furniture which has never been polished becomes more dull. Use the duster also for the window sashes, ledges of the doors, and, in fact, the woodwork generally.

The feather duster saves much time in the *daily* dusting of *bric-a-brac* and light articles, which, however, as I have said, once a week should be moved. The feather duster is a favorite implement with servants and its use is so abused that I have sometimes thought it might be best to interdict its use altogether, when I have seen a maid go round a room and with a feather duster flick the dust from one object to another (removing none, but simply changing its place), and in a few seconds pass out of the room to repeat the operation elsewhere. In its proper place it is invaluable.

PROGRAMME OF WORK.

(FOR GENERAL DAILY WORK SEE PROGRAMME NO. 1.)

SPECIAL WORK FOR FRIDAY.

See to the odds and ends in the larder; try out the week's fat; make broth of bones; make stew or hash of odds and ends of meat.

If fine pastry is needed, make it for use next day.

Sweep the lower floor; give everything a thorough beating and dusting; clean all fine brasses.

Clean windows, mirrors, etc. Dust picture frames with feather duster and replace ornaments.

If weather permits, brush the outside blinds and window sills.

TO CLEAN BRASS.

If the brass is much tarnished, scour first with vinegar and salt, or wood ashes very finely powdered and mixed with water or kerosene. If you use the vinegar, wash with clean hot suds as soon at the tarnish is removed, then polish with whitening and leather, but unless badly stained avoid the acid.

Remember that all metals cleaned with acids tarnish again much more quickly than if cleaned without. For brasses cleaned weekly, a little oil and rottenstone rubbed on, and polished with dry rottenstone, or simply a leather and whitening will be sufficient.

TO CLEAN LIGHT PAINT.

For light colored paint use nothing stronger than warm water and soap. *Always* wipe dry with a clean cloth. This prevents any appearance of smeariness.

TO CLEAN DARK WOOD.

If the woodwork is dark, not painted, but hard finished, go over it with a little oil and turpentine or alcohol mixed, using a hard brush for crevices. If you do not object to the odor, kerosene will do instead of anything else, and pass off in an hour or two.

CHAPTER XII.

SATURDAY is the day on which there is a general finishing up. In households where there is no regular course of work, on this last day of the week there is a great bustle to get everything clean for Sunday. Very often in such cases, everything that can be left undone is crowded into Saturday's work, making it long and arduous. Circumstances have so much to do with cases, that it is almost presumptuous to make any sweeping assertions, and yet, unless there are strong reasons for leaving any work except the kitchen and its appurtenances and the necessary work of the day, for the last day of the week, I think it is bad management.

The kitchen closets should be emptied, the shelves dusted, and then wiped off with a damp cloth, (in summer well washed with strong borax water to prevent ants,) and the papers changed. If you have a servant she will probably hanker—especially if she is German—for the vandyked and perforated paper sold for facing closet shelves; it is well to encourage any love of kitchen adornment, and although you may yourself prefer neat white paper or think home-made vandykes preferable, she will not. The paper is so cheap, it is not worth while to damp enthusiasm by economy in such trifles; but cheap as the paper is, I think the white enameled cloth sold for the purpose, costing more at first, is in the end as cheap and better; it can be washed when soiled, and never hangs in tatters from some accidental rent. Some like the enameled cloth not only to face, but to cover the entire shelf, but unless nailed on, it curls at the edges in a short time; and if nailed, dust, crumbs, and water, all find their way beneath. In summer, you cannot be too careful with kitchen closets. It will seem perhaps unnecessary to have closets in which the things seem quite free from dust, disturbed every week, but prevention is easier than cure, and so very little encouragement will bring that summer plague, the red ant, that it is better to work before they come than to do double work to get clear of them. Should they come in spite of precaution, however, a few whole cloves sprinkled about the shelves is the cleanest and most effectual way of getting rid of them. Black ants are a great pest, but less difficult to get rid of, although as they come in the house with fruit, your cleanliness will not prevent their arrival. Wormwood laid about or the use of Persian insect powder will easily destroy them. One mode of prevention for the country, is to allow all newly-gathered firm fruit to remain out-doors, on the piazza, an hour before the basket is brought into the house.

I have said that the closets must all be turned out and cleaned every week. It depends entirely on the manner of doing, whether this is a great piece of business, keeping the kitchen in a muddle for hours, or a very simple operation, over in an hour or less. Some will go to work, remove the contents of all the closets, cover every table and the floor with them, and while the closets themselves are being cleaned, chaos reigns. I have even known servants to take pride in this upturning, as a proof of their thorough cleanliness ; but the work can be quite as thoroughly done without any such nuisance. Begin with the top shelf, remove all articles to the lower one, dust and wipe the shelf, lay in a sheet of clean paper, dust and replace each article ; then do the same to the other shelves.

All tin bowls, pails, and articles, except those used for baking, should be scoured bright. All coppers, brasses or nickel-plated articles should be also made to shine their brightest. Nothing, after a polished range and bright fire, adds so much to the sense of cheerfulness in a kitchen as bright metals, and certainly nothing speaks so strongly of industry. Let me hasten to say in parenthesis, that although I speak of the appropriate ornament bright utensils are to a kitchen, I by no means think an already over-worked woman should attempt to keep them so— any more than she would keep her children in white dresses because they are pretty. Let such a one be content with the cleanliness that soap and water give, and leave polishing to women who have helping hands.

Before the tables are scrubbed all the cooking should be finished, pie and cake made ; work as far as possible forwarded and prepared for next day. If there is poultry for dinner on Sunday, have it drawn and the giblets, the liver, gizzard, neck, and feet put on to boil for gravy, with a pint of water, a piece of carrot as large as your thumb, a piece of onion (a quarter of a medium-sized one,) a saltspoonful of salt and a quarter one of pepper to each set of chicken or duck giblets ; a quart of water to those of a turkey or goose and double the vegetables. Let them stew very slowly and well covered till the liquid is reduced to half. You will have from each chicken half a pint of strong gravy that will be a jelly next day, *if the feet are used*. This is so seldom done, however, that perhaps it may be well for me to tell how they are cleaned.

Drop the feet, two at a time, into *boiling* water, take one out as quickly as possible, strip the outer skin from it, bend back each nail till it comes off, and the foot will be delicate and white. Do not leave them one moment longer in the water than you can help. The first one will be easiest and the skin leave it almost like a glove ; if you work slowly or let them stand in water, instead of the outer skin coming off it will "set" and can only be got off with the flesh. You will need a coarse cloth and a fork to avoid scalding your hands.

In hot weather, after poultry is drawn, tie some powdered charcoal in a piece of muslin, and leave it inside.

As a rule the actual cleaning of the kitchen should be the last thing. The pantries, larder, refrigerator and cellar all may usually have the weekly cleaning before the kitchen, because in carrying water, and tracking in and out, the clean kitchen will be soiled ; this, however, depends much on the arrangement of the house. I only suggest the order of such work, because I have known inexperienced women to do the wrong thing first, simply from lack of thought. The safe or larder should be washed with water and borax as should the refrigerator ; the last useful contrivance so very easily becomes malodorous, and imparts its odor to the articles kept within it that very special care is necessary. Every other day at least in warm weather it should be wiped out with cold water ; not only the bottom and shelves, but the moisture that condenses on the sides. Once a week wash it with hot water and borax, taking care that every spot is cleansed ; keep charcoal in the corners which change often. But clean as you may be, you will not escape the "refrigerator odor" unless care is taken to let things get nearly cold before putting them in. Fish, bacon, ham, cheese, nor any kind of cooked vegetable should never go into the refrigerator. Bacon and hams are best hung in bags ; fish may be put in a pail with a piece of ice wrapped in newspaper under it, if necessary to keep many hours. Cooked vegetables will keep twenty-four hours in hot weather, if the safe is in a clean, airy place. Every opportunity should be taken of provisions being low and of occasional cool days, when they will keep in the safe, to open the refrigerator doors. Butter, once it has been on ice, cannot be taken from it without injury ; but, if other things favor the airing, it can be arranged like the fish in a pail with ice. If in spite of all, or from unavoidable neglect, the refrigerator does acquire the well known close smell, put a tablespoonful of ground coffee in a shovel or small pan, made very hot, so that the coffee will scorch, but not burn, and set it while smoking in the ice box, and close it ; it will remove all odor and have only for a few hours that of burning coffee.

If you have fortunately a nice boarded or cemented cellar, there will be no trouble with mop and broom in keeping it clean ; if, however, you have a newly built cottage in the suburbs, you may have a cellar which is neither boarded nor cemented. This is a very different matter to keep tidy, and a servant is apt to think such a cellar has no need to be kept clean, that it is indeed a dumping ground for all rubbish.

I have a friend who at the end of a three months illness (during every convalescing week of which she had asked her clean seeming servant if she cleared up the cellar regularly, and warned her never to allow anything to accumulate,) visited, with her first strength, her lower regions and came out appalled ; it seemed to her as if every egg that had been used since she last saw it, had its shells cast down those stairs, all the unused papers lay in dank profusion, discarded lemon rinds, rags, broken crockery; in fact the place looked like the forlorn out-door spots one sees in the neighborhood of shanties. It was winter, and the maid had saved putting her head outdoors to the swill barrel by using the cellar, intending no doubt to have a grand clear up before the lady should be well enough to explore. My friend was thankful she had had no vision of that cellar during her sick days.

If you have a cellar with an earth floor, sprinkle it frequently with fine lime ; keep a box in it, and three or four times a year have half a bushel of unslaked lime put in the box. It will slake in the air and dry it in doing so. The old lime is useful to throw over a refuse heap as an absorbent and is good for the soil. It is a good plan to make every dark corner of an underground cellar light by putting over the soil a thick layer of lime, then if any object finds its way here it will be conspicuous without a light.

The ideal kitchen table is the one scrubbed to ivory whiteness, and as scrubbing seems one of the lost arts, I will give directions for scrubbing properly, because here it is done at all it is often just so much labor wasted. Nice washing with clear soap and water will look quite as well as bad scrubbing ; by this I mean the scrubbing of the average maid, which does her no credit, and yet, if she is industrious and willing, has probably cost her as hard work as if the result had been better. But to a woman whose own hands must compass all the work of the house, and who would naturally be careful of her own possessions, I recommend covering the kitchen table with white enameled cloth ; it will wear a couple of years if neatly nailed on ; boiling water will not mark it, nor will it readily stain. Of course, the use of one of the pot boards recommended in an early chapter will save it greatly, but in truth, I have found that nothing that can be placed on a well-kept kitchen table will hurt the cloth, and fruit, etc., will not stain, as it would the uncovered board. It looks clean and bright while work is going on ; but if the kitchen is used to sit in after work is done, as of course it would be if a maid is kept, a cheerful red and white cloth to throw over it in the afternoon costs little and gives an air of coziness and comfort. So, by the way, does a reflector behind the lamp—especially if it be on a bracket, the light will be much increased, and can be thrown to any desired spot without the danger of carrying the lamp.

Now to the scrubbing. If the table is to be un covered it needs daily scrubbing to keep it white, but if scrubbed daily in the usual way it may get darker day by day. I have said the *usual* way, perhaps I ought to say, "usual" so far as my observation goe' (although I believe in parts of New England the goo' old art of scrubbing is still understood) and explain what that way seems to me.

The average scrubber then has a pail half full of water, brush, soap, and a rag often the waist of an old dress but usually something cotton. Very often the scrubbing brush is applied *first* with just what water flows from it, and it may be used with vigor and good will ; in other cases the cleaning cloth may be wrung nearly dry and passed over the table before the brush is applied, then the brush well soaped is used, the soap and dirt making little waves wherever a brush has been. When the scrubbing is finished, the table has a *dryish* gray lather all over it. The water is well wrung out of the cloth, and the gray lather is wiped

ip with it—*not washed off* as it should be. If the
scrubber is in earnest to have her work right she will
wring her cloth again and rub it over the table once
more. This is the wrong way, yet the effort of the
best intentions.

Now for the right way, by which I mean no arbi-
trary notion of my own, but the way women were
taught to scrub in the days of our grandmothers, when
to have snow-white boards was one of the glories of
housekeeping; this way our mothers often knew,
but probably the general use of carpets and oilcloth
has made the pride in good scrubbing die away, or
center only in the kitchen tables; but the right way
in scrubbing as in other things is the way that produces the best results for the labor expended.

Old flannels of all kinds should be kept for scrubbing and cleaning paint—undervests, drawers, skirts,
all come in for it. In England, where scrubbing is
still the glory of the poorer people, cottagers vying
with each other on the color of their boards, there is
a coarse gray flannel made called "house-flannel,"
expressly for the purpose. Next to flannel, is old
coarse soft linen, old kitchen towels, crash, etc. So
necessary to good cleaning is soft absorbent material,
that I would almost rather my maids destroy articles
of far more value than the scrub cloths, because the
supply is so limited, especially if we give away our
disused underclothing. For this reason keep the supply under your own care, see that after each using the
cloth is dried and not thrown away until it is really
used as long as possible. Many girls will be conscien-

tious about towels and dusters because they have
money value, but cleaning cloths, being *only rag*
they will consider may be thrown aside any time an
fresh ones taken.

In addition to the soft wet cloth a dry rubber (be
made of old Russian crash that has done service f
round or dish towel) should be kept; a scrubbi
brush of hard bristles is best, the soft excelsior brus
are of little use except for coarse paint, and brus
made of broom straw, although not entirely satisf
tory, are about the best one can get when bri
brushes are not to be had, or are too expensive.

Tables that have been neglected may be blea
by spreading on them over night a layer of
ashes, made into a mortar-like paste, with water;
next day brush it off and scrub. The same paste may
be laid on floors when spotted with grease.

TO SCRUB.

Wet your soft cloth, leave *plenty* of water in it,
then wet the table or surface you are scrubbing liberally with it, so that water enough remains to make a
lather; now with the brush *scrub the way of the grain
of the wood* , paying extra attention to all gray spots.
Now rinse the cloth, wring it very little, for you don't
want to *wipe* off, but to *rinse* off, the dirt you have just
scrubbed out; if wiped off, the dirty water is only
smeared over the surface again. Sop up the soapy
lather, then rinse a second time with the water; wring
your cloth as dry as possible and go over it again,
wringing it dry as often as it absorbs water. Last of

all, rub as dry as you can with the dry rubber ; this removes the last of the soiled water and helps the wood to dry quickly, which is a great point in making boards white.

In cleaning floors never wet too large a space at once. If beyond the comfortable range of the arm, there is almost certain to be a dark circle when dry, showing where you leave off each piece ; because, being out of easy reach you have no power to scrub well or wipe dry. Always in using the drying cloth, rub it well *beyond* the space you are now cleaning over, to the one last done.

The use of a little washing soda or borax in the water is excellent for boards, and if they have been neglected a small lump of lime in the water greatly helps to make them white. After tables are scrubbed attend to the sink, put a lump of washing soda as large as an egg at least, over the sink hole, and pour a kettle of boiling water over every part of it, using your sink brush to send it into all greasy parts. When the sink is quite free from grease, wipe off the pump. (If you are fortunate enough to have faucets, they of course would have been polished with the bright things earlier.)

Wash, the last thing before the floor, all finger marks from the paint ; also the chairs if painted ; the backs of them if caned ; the top of the flour barrel and the windows. Be especially careful to clean kitchen window sills ; so many things are put on them, they are more apt to be soiled than any others. Needless to say that floors must *always* be swept before they are washed.

To clean oil cloth, do not scrub it unless it has been badly cleaned many times, when, with the fine corrugated surface now usual, dirt, or rather the dirty water allowed to remain in it will have grimed it so that you will need to use a *soft* brush and scrub the way of the lines; but usually, warm water, one wet and dry cloth are all that are needed. Oil cloth and paint need the wiping with a coarse dry cloth as much as boards, and well repay the extra trouble. Skim milk used in place of water to clean oil cloth gives it brightness and lustre. Painted floors must be treated just as oil cloth is.

I have one thing more to say about the kitchen sink. If you put in a lump of soda weighing half pound or more every day or two, you will have no trouble with the drain pipe becoming clogged with grease. So large a piece will dissolve very slowly, but all the water that goes down will help to cleanse instead of soil the pipe. Whenever you have a kettle of boiling water that you do not need at once, pour it into the sink.

We have now gone through the work of a plain househould for the six working days. Very much more goes to make up that woman's profession, "housekeeping," than the mere work; yet, the order of that, and the way it should be done are perhaps the first things the novice wants to know. In future chapters we will go into such other questions as seem to bear on the questions of housekeeping, the marketing, management of food, and such economies and contrivances as may help the housekeeper of limited means, and some suggestions that may be suitable to the ordering of larger households.

PROGRAMME OF WORK.

(For General Daily Work See Programme No. 1.)

SPECIAL WORK FOR SATURDAY.

The first thing in the morning, thoroughly clean the range, remove all covers, and with a small brush kept for that purpose, sweep from the top of the oven all ashes, soot, etc. Sometimes there are parts where soot will lodge ; a long-handled iron spoon or short trowel as the case may require, will remove such collection better than anything else. Brush off clinging soot wherever you may see it ; a turkey or goose wing is better for this purpose than a brush. When all is clean, black the stove or range. If properly kept there will be very little grease about it. A greasy stove should be washed with strong suds in which washing soda is dissolved; do this over night if you have such a stove to clean. Small grease spots simply require a little dry stove blacking in powder sprinkled over them, and then quick brushing to remove them. If the iron is red and there is trouble in making the blacking adhere, use a teaspoonful of molasses or syrup when you mix the blacking. Mix blacking with water to a thin paste, using the syrup if necessary; rub the range all over with it, taking special care to go into corners, etc., then with a stiff brush begin at the dryest part to polish ; the thinner the blacking is put on the better ; brush vigorously till every part is polished ; slow feeble brushing will leave it a dull black, not a bright one.

Clean out closets, remove everything from one shelf, lay in clean paper, dust and return each article to its place before beginning another. In this way closet cleaning may be carried on without confusion ; even if you are interrupted in the doing, the kitchen will not be encumbered.

When closets are cleansed and re-arranged, scour the tins and clean all copper and brass articles.

TO SCOUR TINS, COPPERS, ETC.

Wash in hot suds then dip a wet rag in fine sifted coal ashes, scour well and then polish with dry ashes. Coppers if much stained can be cleaned with vinegar and salt, or oxalic acid. Put ten cents' worth of acid in a quart of water and bottle. Label *poison* in large letters and keep for use. It is a dangerous article, yet very useful to have at hand. Keep it by itself in some place inaccessible to children.

Oxalic acid will clean all stains from brass or copper, but they require polishing with a dry powder afterwards. Fine ashes are as good as anything, although there are several inexpensive manufactured articles sold for the purpose which are excellent for coarse kitchen utensils. I mention the use of acid in cleaning because it is a quick method of removing tarnish, but I would remind you that if stains are once removed you will have better results by cleaning without it, as after its use the brightness so quickly passes off. For articles regularly cleaned, therefore, I prefer the use of kerosene and wood ashes ; if the odor of kerosene is offensive, any cheap oil will answer. Wet a rag in oil, dip it in the ashes and go all over the surface of the copper, then dip a dry rag in the dry ashes and polish. Soap and sand may be used to scour tins if preferred to ashes, but must not be used on copper; the sand is too coarse.

Clean all the entries, pantries, laundry, etc. Wash the shelves of the safe or larder with hot water and soda or borax ; clean the refrigerator in the same way, going all over the inside ; put fresh pieces of charcoal in the corners ; air if it be possible. Wash out the bread box, stand it in a hot place to dry thoroughly. Wash the finger marks from the kitchen paint, clean windows and sills, scrub the tables, clean up the cellar, and when all other work is done, wash or scrub the kitchen floor and stoop or piazza, or whatever may be the outside appurtenances.

TO SCRUB.

Use plenty of hot water and soap; a small piece of washing soda as large as a hickory nut, or a teaspoonful of borax in it helps the work. Use the brush always the way of the grain of the wood ; take care to not scrub with the board only just moistened; use plenty of water. *Rinse* off the dirty water and dry by rinsing your cloth through, and wring it two or three times, finally wipe with a coarse dry cloth.

TO WASH BOARDS.

Follow just the same process with the exception of using the brush. Wet the surface thoroughly first, then rinse the cloth, soap it, and wash the surface ; rinse, not wipe, off this soapy water, rinsing and wringing out the cloth dry as you can and wipe—finally go over with the drying towel. See full directions, Chapter XII.

This latter process for those who lack strength, is far better than bad scrubbing; the boards will keep clear and of a good color.

TO CLEAN OIL CLOTH OR PAINTED FLOORS.

Oil cloth should not have much water used on it ; keep it clear by rinsing the cloth several times. Dry with a drying cloth. If skim milk is plentiful, use it for painted floors or oil cloth in preference to water.

CHAPTER XIII.

HOUSEKEEPING ON A LARGE SCALE—SERVANTS—MARKET-
ING, KITCHEN FARE, ETC.

HITHERTO these papers have been considering chiefly the needs of those housekeepers who either work unassisted, or with one servant. In this paper I propose to discuss management for larger households. The actual work to be done differs only as to its divisions among several hands. The work to be done is the same, and done in the same way, only there is probably much more of it. In a house where three servants are required, there is often as much work on the lower floor alone as in a small house. The division of work is often a difficult matter; for servants who profess to do one kind of work, do not like to share that of any other servant, although their own work may not be sufficient to keep them employed, and the one they are expected to help may be kept very busy. Thus the chambermaid and waitress does not like to help the nurse; the laundress, even if the family washing is all out of the way before Friday, objects to sweep or nurse or wait, and the cook will decline to do anything out of her own province, and yet, unless your family is so large, or you live in such a way as to warrant the employment of a full staff of servants, some such doubling of duties must be, therefore when you engage, have a very well defined understanding on the point.

Many ladies are vague as to what each maid will be required to do beyond what she may consider her own work, and maids will often engage to do what they really mean to shirk as far as possible.

A distinct understanding at first, and an intimation that each servant will be held responsible for the work she has undertaken, is the best way to avoid the annoyance of disputes between servants later.

It is well to have a list of the weekly duties of each servant, which you read to her when engaged; have a copy of this list for each. If possible, write the list in the order in which you wish the work done. It will be an assistance to the servants, and dispute be impossible between themselves, or any excuse for misunderstanding of orders, only, let everything of this sort be done at the very beginning. Of course you can avoid doing this unpleasantly, and a servant who would take umbrage at what is for her own assistance, is not one who will be worth regretting the loss of, for it will show she lacks sense.

DIVISION OF WORK.

The division of the work is the question on which many housekeepers are in doubt, and it is very difficult to give rules that will apply to all cases; the presence of an invalid in the family, the fact that the children are all very young, perhaps an infant, with the one older only able to toddle, or many other things, may cause any given set of rules to be quite useless. But every woman must judge for herself whether her house presents any exception to general rules and arrange accordingly.

In a family where there is a plain cook, chambermaid and nurse, the cook will do the family washing; if it is large, the chambermaid should assist while the cook gets the meals, which without being makeshift, should be as simple on that day as possible, but parenthetically, I will say that many think by having steak or chops and vegetables they are saving the cook; really a roast joint is far less hindrance and trouble. Sometimes the chambermaid cooks breakfast and lunch; this I do not think a good plan. The really better way, if economy is not rigidly necessary, is, if the washing is too much for the cook to do and attend to the meals for that day, to have a woman to assist. This leaves the chambermaid free to do her usual work, and on Monday, as I have elsewhere said, a general picking up and dusting is advisable; she will also be as neat as usual to answer the door and wait at table. With the ironing she can assist the cook after her usual work on Tuesday. Of course if you are fortunate enough to find and can afford to pay, a thoroughly good cook, she cannot be expected to do more than her own and the kitchen washing, by which I mean the towels, cloths, dusters, etc. If your table requires the services of an expert cook, she would have no time. But although I fully recognize the right of a woman who has really fitted herself to take a place as an excellent cook (by which I mean that she can make fine soups, *entrees,* sauces, and pastry without your superintendence) to receive high wages and be exempt from washing, I deprecate such conditions being given, as they often are, to a woman who is really only a better kind of general servant (sometimes not a *better* kind). I remember visiting a friend, who said in course of conversation:

"I believe I'm going to have peace now. I have engaged a first-class cook. I have to pay her $25 a month, but then she knows her work without my going down to oversee everything that is not of the simplest kind. I've been almost worn out. Of course she won't do the washing, I must put that out, but I'll economize in every other way to make up."

I congratulated my friend on her resolve; she was not strong, and with the table she enjoyed having for her husband, it did not seem to me that the $25 or so a month which the extra wages and washing would cost, was ill spent. The new cook arrived, my friend ordered a simple dinner,—vermicelli soup, breaded cutlets, roast chicken and apple pie. The new cook said, reading the list,

"How do you make the vermicelli soup, ma'am?"

Alas! for my friend's hopes. However, a recipe was handed to her and she was left to her own devices.

The soup at dinner was fairly good family soup, not at all clear, with vermicelli broken in it; evidently she did not know how it should have been. The cutlets were a sorry spectacle; they had been breaded, but the bread had refused to remain on. The chicken was fairly roasted, and the pie, a good one for a family of children; the crust looked like paper, was about a quarter of an inch thick, *hemmed* all round the edge and pricked over with a fork. In fact the dinner was just such as a good general servant, or plain cook, at $14 a month would have served.

The moral of this little story is that while I would not grudge high wages for good work, I would strongly object to pay them unless I was sure I was not rewarding the self-assertion of an ignorant person. Some time I hope to go into this subject more fully, for I believe very much more of the servant difficulty depends on this point than most people think.

With regard to the servants' washing; unless a laundress forms part of your establishment, when, of course, she will do that of the whole family, the chambermaid and nurse will do their own, each at such times as you may fix for them. The chambermaid takes care of the children while the nurse washes, and she can iron in the evening. If your children are very young and the nurse takes entire charge, it is better to arrange, when you engage the cook, for her to wash for the nurse, and let the latter do the children's flannels, laces, etc.

The chambermaid, of course, takes charge of the whole upper part of the house, waits at table, cleans silver, is responsible for the front steps, door and vestibule, and washes the glass, silver and fine china; the greasy dishes go down to the cook.

If an indoor man servant is kept he relieves the chambermaid of many of these duties. He takes charge of the butler's pantry, washing all china and glass, cleans silver, waits at table and, if you engage him as waiter, and pay him the wages for a good one, he should be a good carver, able to prepare salads, and understand the service of wines, etc.

The chambermaid, relieved of table duties, may be expected to help the nurse, so that she may sew, or you may prefer to leave the nurse to her duties, letting her keep the children's clothes in order, while the baby sleeps, and the chambermaid you may require to keep the house linen in order or assist in some other way.

One thing be sure to do. Have everything very clearly defined in your own mind, just what you want done and whom you want to do it, before attempting to arrange with your servants ; any doubt or vagueness *you* may have in giving directions, will surely be reflected in their actions.

I have heard ladies say, " I can't make such conditions *before* I engage servants ; they would not come to me." This is, I am sure, a mistake. Many servants will agree to more than they intend to carry out, and very few who are worth having would refuse a place because you make your conditions known to them, provided they are reasonable, but if they are engaged without the clear understanding, you very likely will have trouble after ; they will probably look on all they are asked to do outside of their special duties as an imposition.

A successful housekeeper of my acquaintance always engaged her three servants with the proviso that they *might* be required to cook, to wash, to wait at table, to do, in short, anything that they were asked ; in fact she engaged them all as general servants, although she divided the work of her house as other people do. I don't recommend the experiment, I only mention it because she never had more difficulty in finding servants to take her place than other people ; if some refused, others accepted, and more willing servants or a better ordered house I never saw.

Of course really expert servants will not engage in this way, but there are very few of them, and they require very high wages, which, *if they are* what they profess to be, will generally be cheerfully paid.

Where the servants are as many or nearly as many as the family, it is more economical to have a separate table ; especially is this the case where the heads of the family like small dishes, such as birds, *entrees,* etc., etc. But not only is it advisable from the point of economy, but it makes the evening work lighter. The servants have their tea at five or half past five, the cook and waitress then have nothing to do but to wash up after the family dinner, while if they wait until the family have dined before they get their meal, it makes very late work. With an intelligent and obliging cook every one is more comfortable with this arrangement.

The most economical and satisfactory way of carrying out this plan is for the kitchen dinner to form the family luncheon. This saves cooking two mid-day meals and ensures contentment, for what is good enough for your own eating will not be objected to by your servants, as, with their over-sensitiveness as a class, might be the case.

For those who may not be experienced in this plan of housekeeping, I will give a few bills of fare intended to combine the family lunch and servants' dinner. On days that such viands as corned beef or roast pork are recommended, if there are young children dining, there may be a chop for each provided, a little finely chopped steak made into cakes and broiled, or there may have been some little thing left from your own evening dinner that can be nicely prepared. It is in these small things that your good management will be shown.

I want to say here that I do not think it right or good economy to buy poor food for the kitchen, but if you have a family of hearty working people to provide for, you will be wise to buy such parts of meat as will cut to the best advantage; but although for this purpose, what may be called the prime cuts will not be purchased, the meat itself should be of the best quality. Indeed, an inferior joint of fine beef or mutton is better eating than the choicest cuts of inferior meat.

Abundance of good, nourishing, palatable food is what those who work require, and no one will hesitate to say that a hearty meal, a well cooked chuck roast, although it may cost only fourteen cents a pound, is better food than the remains of say a pair of chickens or a quarter of young lamb, after serving five or six people up stairs. Yet when the kitchen family is expected to dine after the dining-room, sometimes a very scanty repast remains, not because sufficient money is not expended, but because the viands are of an unsuitable kind. I am so anxious not to be misunderstood on this point, not to be supposed to advocate a stinted housekeeping, that I want to make it quite plain that I do not advocate your providing as if for an inferior class of beings, but just as the keeper of a boarding house or large school would provide.

I have known ladies sensitive on this point who would say, "I like my servants to live just as well as I do. I give them the same as we eat ourselves," and buy seven or eight pounds of spring chicken for a family of ten,—five up stairs and five down; the cost would be from $3 to $4, and, at best of times, the kitchen would get a slight meal of a dainty, at which they grumbled, but as this particular family were living in the city, unexpected visitors to lunch were frequent, and then imagine the debris that would go into the kitchen. Granted that there was a little fish or soup besides to eke it out, and vegetables, so that no one need go hungry, the grumbling and discontent was the same, and the grumblers felt stinted, and yet abundant roast beef or mutton might have been bought for less money.

MARKETING.

Then your marketing must be according to the season. I would not advise an inexperienced woman to go down to Fulton or Washington market alone to provide for her family, if she lives in New York, but I would suggest that a few lessons in marketing be taken from one of the teachers of cooking who have classes for this purpose ; the money expended would be saved over and over again in a very short time. Some gentlemen understand the markets admirably, and when they are willing to send up supplies their wives are very fortunate.

To either the housekeeper who has taken lessons, or the fortunate one with a husband skilled in such matters, I would say, watch the market prices and buy accordingly.

Sometimes turkeys are as cheap as any other good meat. In spring, lamb, of course, should not be bought for hungry people, but in fall, forequarter of lamb is only twelve cents the pound, and is substantial food without being so fat as mutton. Leg of mutton at fourteen cents is cheaper than forequarter at twelve, because it is all meat.

And now, as I shall give in the bills of fare roast pork, let me say a few words about that meat.

In this country, where it is the cheapest of all meat, roast pork is often a rarely used and despised dish, except by Germans and Irish. In English cities, where pork is the most expensive meat, a loin costing more per pound than sirloin of beef, where pork sausages are twenty-two cents to twenty-four cents a pound, while beef sausages (a favorite dish with London working people) are twelve cents to sixteen cents, pork is looked upon as a great treat. Is it only because it is cheap here that it is despised? I know many believe it to be unwholesome ; is not this, too, partly prejudice ? There are some people certainly who *cannot* eat pork, but there are also some to whom veal is almost poison. As to its wholesomeness, I think we ought to look at the people who almost live on it—the English agricultural population, the Germans, who in their various sausages eat it in all forms. Where are there healthier people than those English or those Germans? look at the children who, from the time they are weaned, eat daily such fat pork as would make one shudder to think of ; in English rural districts it is not an occasional, but a steady diet, day after day all the year round. At the roadside, sitting on the mossy banks that flank the fields they are tilling, may be seen laborers with a hunch of bread and a thick slice of pork or of bacon on the top of it, solid fat, and a "thumb piece" (a small piece of bread that the thumb rests on), while they cut down through fat and bread with their knives. This, with perhaps a raw onion and a drink of beer, is their daily dinner year in and year out, but do you suppose they know any thing of dyspepsia ? I don't think many of them ever heard the word, and one look at the ruddy skin, the strong frames even of their old people will tell you that. Of course the outdoor life makes a difference, but the school children are the rosiest and chubbiest. Take at random any group of these pork fed children and there will not be a sickly one among them.

When these girls and boys go to London, as in these days most do, they take places where there is abundant fresh meat; fare such as they never dreamed of, and the one thing they crave is their country pork, not that pork is not eaten in London, but it is expensive, and is not the "pickled" pork with several inches of fat, they love so well. In the baskets of country women visiting city friends, is always a piece of this pickled pork and sometimes a piece of bacon is packed and brought away in a trunk.

To the London working classes, roast leg or loin of pork stuffed, is the next luxury to roast goose, and the working people, if they cannot afford a goose, take pork and sage and onions for a Christmas dinner as the next best thing, roast beef or mutton being the usual Sunday dinner and therefore not a "treat."

I suppose there are no hardier, healthier races in the world than the English and Germans, especially the country people ; both are largely pork fed.

I should perhaps state that I speak only from observation. I have no scientific knowledge on the subject. Pork takes its place in my family in change with other meats, and we know nothing of dyspepsia, which we might do if the American climate made the use of pork unadvisable.

Another thing urged against pork is that the pig is an uncleanly feeder, but no one says this of that dainty bird the chicken. Is there any filth a pig would eat that a chicken would not ? Do not chickens revel in offal ? Can there be a more uncleanly feeder ? If it is the food of the animal that unfits it for use, then the chicken must come under that ban.

I know people who tell me they have never eaten fresh roast pork. If there are any among my readers who do not yet know the excellence of roast leg of pork with the crackling neatly scored and crisped, stuffed with bread, sage and boiled onions, and eaten with apple sauce, let her buy one, and roast it till it is brown as a chestnut, and perhaps she will thank me for persuading her. Perhaps in her house Mrs. Poyser's "stuffed chine" may come to hold a place of honor as a savory joint to have on hand.

I have said thus much on the pork question, because I would like to set people thinking on this cheap and good meat and ask themselves how far their dislike of pork in any other form than ham or bacon comes from knowledge, and how much from prejudice against it as a vulgar dish. It is not, of course, elegant, any more than is roast goose, but it is very toothsome. One word more about it, *it must be thoroughly cooked.* Half an hour to the pound is not too much to allow.

BILLS OF FARE FOR FAMILY LUNCHEON AND KITCHEN DINNER.

1. Roast beef (second joint rib roast is excellent), mashed turnips, baked potatoes, cottage pudding, foaming sauce.

2. Soup, cold roast beef, canned corn or tomatoes, potatoes mashed and browned (salad for dining-room), pickles down stairs, apple pie.

3. Roast leg of mutton, stewed onions, potatoes browned under meat, rice pudding.

4. Corned beef, cabbage, carrots, potatoes, baked Indian pudding. A little dish of minced mutton with rice border, from the cold mutton makes a nice children's dish.

5. Soup (made from bones of roast beef and mutton with a ten cent soup bone), cold corned beef (salad for up stairs), pickles or cold slaw, bread pudding, lemon sauce.

6. Roast pork, sweet potatoes, rice, apple sauce, waffles or a boiled pudding.

Of course I only give these bills of fare in the way of suggestion. Each housekeeper knows the peculiarities of her own family, and can avoid such viands as are objected to. I have given such food as suits the winter months, for which reason I have put salad for up stairs only, as it is in winter costly. However plain this fare may seem for luncheon, I think it will be found preferable to the chops and steaks which are too often depended upon, and which leave no margin for unexpected visitors. With a substantial roast joint on the table, no one can take you by surprise and you will not be wondering what will be left for down stairs, if you know you have only ordered just about enough chop or steak for the family. And even with a dish of cold meat, a soup and a salad, if all be prettily served (that, of course, you must insist on), the meat cut very thin and garnished, you will not need to blush for your table.

I have in my mind a family of eight, four up stairs and four down. In buying a roast of beef for such a family it is cheaper to buy one of twelve pounds and to cut off the flat end and have it corned, than one of eight and roast it whole. The end piece, corned and pressed, is very nice for kitchen tea or breakfast, while the solid nine pounds or so you have roasted is all available meat. If there is only partly enough of any joint for the second day's dinner, it may be made up with fish or Hamburg steak; Hamburg steak is the juicy side of the round steak chopped very fine, all gristle removed, made into cakes an inch thick, highly seasoned and broiled. (If the chopping is done at the butcher's you will be likely to get the veiny side of the round instead of the tender one).

Of course you will instruct your cook that she must carve the meat for dinner down stairs just as carefully as it is done up stairs. I have seen a fine sirloin roast leave the dining-room with only the tenderloin eaten, and after the kitchen dinner of four persons, there was nothing but the flap end, the bone and a strew of hacked bits of meat. Each had been allowed to hack a piece off—cutting across the joint and rejecting every morsel but the solid lean.

The cook is mistress of the kitchen and should preside at the table. If possible a room off the kitchen should be appropriated for the meals, and every proper article provided for comfort. This room cannot always be allowed, but insist that the table be laid properly, and that the cook serve the meals hot and comfortable. Some cooks are very disagreeable on this point; if they are, you will surely have discontent among the other servants.

KITCHEN BREAKFAST.

Give the cook to understand that cold roast joints are never to be touched the first day, either to make hash or be cut for kitchen breakfast; a nice com-

fortable woman will save her odds and ends and once
or twice a week make a stew or hash, but you may
have some such rule as this:

MONDAY—Eggs (if cheap).
TUESDAY—Fish balls.
WEDNESDAY—Sausage.
THURSDAY—Ham or bacon.
FRIDAY—Picked up cod.
SATURDAY—Liver.
SUNDAY—Stewed beef kidney.

Baked potatoes, or hot cakes or corn bread each
morning; where there is a cow, oatmeal, etc.

Of course often the remains of two joints will make
hash.   On your daily visit to the larder or safe, you will
see what remains there are and suggest to your cook
such use, if she is not quick at such things.   If you
interest yourself to see that your servants have the
comfort you intend, it will generally ensure it, and if
the cook will not take the trouble to make the best use
of things for her fellow servants sake, discharge her.

Allow for the kitchen a certain amount of tea for
the week, assure yourself that it is *ample,* and then
give the cook to understand that it is to last.   Let it
be of good quality, for a servant's tea is a great comfort ; without some limit, however, it is one of the
things often greatly wasted.   As I said, be sure there
is no stint in your household, but let it be known that
you know exactly how far things should go and that
you notice any excess.   There seems to be a ten-
dency among servants, when they get where there is

an abundance, to revel in waste, everything is used profusely, and this is especially the case with those who have never known what plenty was. You must therefore, impress them with the knowledge that although you allow plenty, you tolerate no waste.

With regard to the kitchen tea. If there has been meat twice before in the day, bread and butter and cheese with baked apples or stewed dried fruit in winter, fresh fruit in summer are sufficient. When eggs are cheap, if you choose, they may be used, or the before named pressed boiled beef may be used, or in place of the fruit you may choose to keep a ham or a piece of cold meat (cold stuffed chine) to cut on, the cook of course, cutting it, and seeing that it is properly used. If you are dining out, hot cakes or waffles may be indulged in without interfering with the dinner. I should have stated before that the chambermaid usually prepares the table for tea.

A supply of pickles, spiced fruits, etc., should be put up in summer and fall if possible for the kitchen; when it is not done it is well to buy them, giving a bottle out from time to time. Such things do not cost much, and add much to the comfort and contentment of those who serve you. Of course the costlier imported articles, canned vegetables, etc., are kept for dining-room use ; you give them out as they are wanted.

Whatever remains of your evening dinner will not be touched after it leaves the table unless there is some perishable dish you do not wish kept, such as certain jellies or ice-cream, etc. The cook is responsible for the meat, the waiter or waitress for fruits, olives, confectionery, etc.

It is here that you will find the advantage of the middle day dinner. The children will probably have had tea with the nurse, and if not in bed will only come down to a light dessert. With soup, a little piece of fish, a partridge or chicken or sweetbreads, an *entree* (if your cook can compass it), salad, cheese, and dessert, you have a dainty little dinner, and if you have either of the birds named, and there are only two to dine, you have a salmi or fricassee as *entree* for next night, or else a breakfast dish. Also if the fish is not all used, it will serve up with white sauce and chopped eggs, or else can be scalloped; this can be done if only two good tablespoonfuls remain. Having provided excellently for your kitchen, you will have no scruple in ordering everything of this sort to be saved, or inquiring for it if it does not appear.

CHAPTER XIV.

I SPOKE in the last chapter about the advisability of providing substantial fare for the kitchen. Very many shrink from doing this with some sort of feeling that it is mean to do it. Especially is this the case where the housekeeper has for some years of her life perhaps, kept only one servant. Naturally, in such a case the maid lives as the family does—to make a distinction in the food of one person would be more trouble than profit, and therefore not necessary on the score of economy, and yet even here, much depends on the servant. A self-respecting young woman who would use our luxuries as we used them, may safely be left to her own discretion, and to help herself to cake or preserves, or whatever dainties we affect, and ourselves be saved the business, so annoying to a sensitive housekeeper, of laying restrictions. I have known in my experience more servants who did not abuse such freedom than those who have abused it; but when, either from ignorance or greediness, such liberty cannot be given, the line must be firmly drawn even for one. When a can of peaches or choice preserves, only one-third or less used in the dining-room, is emptied at one meal in the kitchen, or a pot of jelly, just opened and a spoonful or two used, is seen no more, the cake eaten in place of bread—in short, when it is evident Delia makes the luxuries the staple part of her food, she must be, humiliating as it is to do it—"allowanced," the saucer of preserve apportioned, the piece of cake, or the pickles laid aside, and the remainder put away, or, in the case of rare dainties, the rich pound cake kept only for "highdays and holidays," or the candies, macaroons, choice fruit, which the *right* kind of a girl would understand are to be left unless specially given to her, you must, if you have the *wrong* girl, put away yourself. Servants in large families know this; indeed if she did but know it, the one maid in a small cottage, who shares everything with the master and mistress thereof, comes in for more of the good things of life than her compeer in the elegant mansion, where although there may be every comfort, there must be less of the freedom of home than in a small family.

The general servant who will not bear the least rebuke for neglect of duty, from the kind mistress of a small house, will work hard and cheerfully, take fault-finding meekly, and often, if the lady is an over economical manager, fare badly if the house is in Fifth avenue or of similar distinction. Then again with the servants in hotels, there is often, I am told, despite the abundance and the waste of the dining-room, a severe economy exercised in the victualing of the large staff of servants who never taste the best quality of anything. This I do not know from personal observation, but I do know that the chambermaids, scrubbing girls, etc., at one first-class hotel where I was staying a few years ago, had their sleeping quarters in dark airless cubby holes, that in no private family would be considered possible to use as rooms under any consideration. It made one ill to think of what those closets must have been in hot weather. The mistress of a private family, if she had to ask her maid to unmake a bed or change the arrangements of a room after the day's work was done, would be full of regret, sometimes a little afraid to tell her necessity, and although Delia may be good natured enough about it for once, she certainly would not like her evenings disturbed a second or third time, although her light daily work will not have fatigued her; but the hotel servant, or indeed those in a large boarding-house, will cheerfully obey the order to make ready three or four rooms just vacated, change mattresses and bedsteads perhaps to other rooms, and this at the end of a day in which every minute has been full of work. How account for these things ? Is it that human nature is meek under the conditions of a hard toilful life, and rebellious under better fortune?

It is very curious, and perhaps matter for thought, as explaining the reason why women will be bullied and ground down and defrauded by a firm, or bullied, ill-fed and miserably housed as servants in a hotel, and bear it meekly, who yet would rebel at the mild objurgation of a private employer.

When I began this little talk about the peculiarities of servants, I meant to point out that though we may choose to provide the same food for kitchen and dining-room with one or two servants, in providing a separate table, if with a larger household it be found desirable, there is no meanness, if the table be one that will better supply the substantial food required for manual work than the lighter fare adapted to sedentary life.   Nor is there any meanness in insisting that due economy shall be exercised.   No great business establishment, hotel, steamboat, or any other requiring the providing of food for a great number of employes, could be properly carried on without such regulations as prevent waste.

Before dismissing the servant question, I would be understood as advocating, where means are ample, the employment of sufficient servants to do the work without worry to the mistress, and paying for efficiency if it is to be got.   Often a woman with wide social duties, a large house and a family with two or three children, will be quite as worried and worn out physically, as another poorer woman with one inadequate servant and several children, who wonders what her wealthier neighbor with three servants can find to do.   I will tell her.   She has three servants, but she ought perhaps to have four, because the nurse's time is of course required entirely for the children.   Her husband, because he can give his wife this beautiful house and servants, naturally expects to have good dinners and very many other things that a poorer man equally well able to enjoy them, knows he must do without.   If his wife does her best with his small income she can do no more.   The seeming more easily placed woman has to supplement perhaps each of her maids, her cook is what has come to be understood as "a plain cook," which means too often that she can make one soup, can put meat in the oven and make a very poor pie or pudding. If more is wanted, if dressing for poultry that shall be something more than a wet pudding, flavored (sometimes not) with pepper, salt and onion, the lady must make it herself, or stand by (far more fatiguing to nerves, although the better plan) while it is being made. She must make any but plain cake, and often to help the cook through, she does even that, pastry too, and any little nicety that may be wanted for dinner she must make. If the chambermaid is busy she helps her (and if the family consists of six or seven beside servants, the chambermaid will be busy very often), and then the mistress lays the table, dusts the fine things, often sweeps, makes beds—anything to help through, so that each week the work may be done and not allowed to lap over. The nurse does (perhaps) some sewing, the mistress does the rest ; she, too, often thinks that having several servants, she ought not to employ a seamstress except at times of great pressure ; if she is one of the women who like to have dainty surroundings from children's clothes to the odds and ends about the house, she will find her needle always busy, but in addition to this, just because she is well off, she will have many calls on her time of which her less prosperous neighbor would know nothing. She is asked to do charitable or church work as well as give money, and with many such woman this work is one of the most onerous of duties. Then, because she has a large house, she probably has many visitors, and is expected to receive calls and to make them. The last, however, if systematically done, need not be a severe tax. The *receiving*, unless she has strength of character enough to have an open afternoon, and adhere to it, refusing herself to all casual callers, (a very difficult thing to do without giving offence, yet it should not be so) is a great devourer of time. The endeavor to do all these things, and the many others I have not specified, which every woman will know for herself, is what wears this well-to-do fortunate housekeeper out, and sends her to bed at night quite as weary as a woman with one servant or none.

Perhaps some will say, "I can't see it; I do all these things, I make calls, receive them, make my children's clothes and do church work, and have one servant." And to such a one I reply: Do you also live in a large house, not only are there more rooms, be it remembered, but a large house means—broad corridors, wide stairs, many windows, often large down stairs premises, corridors, laundry, pantries, etc., the surface space of which alone would cover the whole of that in a small house, and every foot has to be kept clean, and then although a woman of small means may do her full share of charitable work, she is is not called upon to help in all sorts of outside directions, as a woman of large means is; if called upon, it is not her duty as it is that of a wealthier woman to do it, nor can she in her smaller house receive frequent staying company, nor would she (at least she ought not) imitate the style of living of the other woman.

To return to the wearing cares of the mistress of a large household in this country, they surely ought not to be ; the cares incidental to small means, and much to do with them, cannot be avoided ; but the woman of large means surely need not have her time absorbed by supplementing her servants. Probably much of this arises from a mistaken sense of duty. One more servant in her household might make the difference ; she knows it, yet feels because other women with as large houses manage with the three or four, that she ought to do so, but often the employment of a laundress so far relieves both cook and chambermaid, that they each get through the work without the mistress's helping hand, or if her time is most consumed at the sewing machine, then one who will be seamstress and waitress may solve the difficulty in a measure, and think, if you are sufficiently well off to live as I am supposing, how very little the wages will be to you after all. Two hundred dollars a year to a woman who has not a thousand to live on, is a vast sum, but to one who would give it for a gown or sack or one piece of furniture, I say go without one gown or economize some other way to release yourself, your nerves, and your time for your children and husband, and for the sake of a blooming old age.

I am far from advocating self-indulgence or idleness, but the strenuous, anxious housekeeper, who puts her own hand to everything without actual need to do it, is by no means the best one, often because she does so much herself she cannot superintend so successfully as she should. I think it may be taken as a rule that the housekeeper who goes through every department of her house daily, who gives her orders for the work to be done, who reads her recipe to her cook, and after once superintending, lets her know that she will be expected to work alone in future, is better served, and the wheels of the domestic machinery go better, than when she executes it herself.

It is said by many that servants are a necessary evil ; therefore, the more you have of them, the worse you are off. This is not quite so. If you can afford to divide your work so that each servant is responsible only for her own department, and you are willing to pay good wages, you have more chance of obtaining ambitious, well-trained servants than if you must engage those who are willing to multiply themselves. We may object to the idea that the woman to whom we pay good wages and give a comfortable home should refuse to take a place where she has to be generally useful, nevertheless object as we may, the fact remains, skilled labor anywhere and everywhere can afford to be independent, and I for one, would not grudge it the right. What I and every other housekeeper ought to object to, is that the half-skilled or quite unskilled servants who absorb our time and too often ruin our health, should either be paid the wages or demand the privileges of the skilled.

In this chapter it may not be out of place to say a few words on any subject that touches women's leisure or means of economizing time, although at a first glance that of calls and visiting days may seem to be more appropriate to a book of etiquette. But in fact the branch of the subject I am about to touch upon, has a very important bearing on housekeeping. I allude to the waste of time consumed in receiving calls, and I want to urge every woman who has any but very intimate friends to have an afternoon in the week to receive calls. Many women of wealth and social position have adopted the fashion, perhaps at first because it was a fashion, but there is a great deal more than that to be said in its favor, and it is the busy woman, who has every moment occupied with household duties and yet keeps her hold on social life, who will find it a saving of time and a means of snatching some passing pleasure and repose from what otherwise is an occasional vexation, whom the custom would help most. The advantage of a receiving day is often fully understood, but women who make no social pretension shrink from it for fear of being thought "airy" or aping fashion, but it is just these women who might look on it as au absolute duty to themselves, and a real kindness to their friends.

How many of us know what it is to have an acquaintance, who is both agreeable and, would be, welcome, call on us just as we are doing something that we are nervously anxious to finish, or that requires our undivided attention ; fortunate if we are not in the middle of some delicate cooking that will spoil by leaving it. There are then but two things to do—ask our visitor right into the kitchen or work room, or leave everything and go to her just as we are; anything is better than to keep her waiting. If we do the first, she will know that she has come just at the wrong time, and feel that she is intruding in spite of your assurance that you wish her to stay, and in fact if you go on busily with your occupation you really cannot enjoy her visit, while if you leave everything, you will show the marks perhaps of being very busy, and your mind will wander to the oven that was just right, and is now cooling, or the work that you wanted to finish so specially to-day ; in any case, you do not enjoy the visit, and your visitor will feel that you have been very polite, but that she might have chosen a better time.

By having a " day " you do away with all this, and you save time.   You know the afternoon or evening when your friends will call, and you arrange accordingly.   You need lose time only for that day ; you will have no exacting work in hand ; you will be dressed and ready, and stocking darning or small mending, although not parlor work, may be left to pick up and can be put away without mental anxiety when visitors arrive.   If you have made it known that you have given up this day, (and you can pleasantly also give your reasons) you may have several calls at one time, while otherwise each would have come separately and separately taken your time. Your callers will probably enjoy meeting each other, and you, with your mind quite free, will be at your best.

The objections to this reception day do not compare with its advantages.   They are, first, that it is sometimes impossible to foresee what we may have to do ; that the very day we have agreed to stay at home is the one on which it will seem almost necessary to go out. Second, that although we have a day, no one comes that day, but on every one but that, so we sacrifice the day in vain.

To the first, the only answer is that we can have no great advantage without some drawback, that you can to a certain extent avoid trouble by carefully considering the matter before choosing your day, think over everything that is for and against it. In cities, one of the things to be avoided as far as possible, is selecting a day on which many of our friends themselves receive. To the second objection I would say, if it is known that you devote one afternoon to receiving your friends, nothing but the most urgent necessity could justify any one in calling at any other time. To do this is a positive rudeness. I have known women not otherwise ill-bred to say : "I know it is not your day, but I so seldom come to this neighborhood I thought I might venture, etc." The lady has not intended to be rude, but it is rude, for if any one comes with real desire to see you, they will even to their own inconvenience, come when they know you are at home ; if they come at another time, it argues that they do not care to see you, but simply to discharge a social duty; this can be done equally well by any one, on merely formal footing, by leaving a card without disturbing you. If there is some urgent object or reason to ask you to receive a call, it should be written on the card, sent in, and if this is not done, no thinking woman should take offense by your excusing yourself. At present it is only in large cities, and there by well-bred people, that the importance of respecting the reception day, in other words, the most precious thing we have—our leisure, is recognized. In places where it is not the general custom, many women try to have "a day," and because for a few weeks, no one or few come on it, and they do come on other days, they become discouraged, disregard their day, go out upon it, or if callers come are obviously unready to receive them.

If you tell your acquaintance that you have a day, you are bound as a lady to be at home; it is one of the excuses of people who do not observe "days," that it's no use putting themselves out to do so, for "Mrs. So and So is always out on her day," they having called once perhaps and found her so, but even once should not have happened. If you do not observe your own rule, no one else will. If some imperative reason calls you out, ask some lady to receive for you; she will explain. Those of your callers who have walked will rest and get cool, or warm, as the season may be. There is another aspect under which you may look at this question, even, if (as some will say) you have not a sufficiently large circle to justify a receiving day. If you have only three or four occasional visitors, it will be a kindness for you to let them know there is a certain hour and day when you will be found at home. How often we come in and find some one we would so gladly have seen has called in our absence, perhaps some elderly or weak person, who has taken a long walk and consequently needed rest.

I hope I have said enough to make some of my readers think over this question seriously, not as an affectation or fashion, but as a means of avoiding one of the smaller worries. It is worry, not work that wears, and I really believe small worries are more injurious in the long run than real trouble; such as we by firmness can remove from our lives, it is our duty to do. No one woman can do much perhaps to change an existing state of things, but if no one woman ever began any social movement, how little would be done!

I have spoken thus far of the setting apart of two or three hours of each week or each two weeks to see callers instead of giving up odd hours all through the week, as one means of saving time and worry, and tried to show that instead of it being a fashionable affectation it is more advisable for the woman who is not fashionable, but a busy housewife, most advisable of all to the one "who does her own work," if she has any social leaning. Now I will say a few words of the custom in its social aspect.

It is somewhat a growing fashion in the city to make the weekly reception a sort of informal festivity; this, if *very simply* done, is a pleasant social custom ; if merely a cup of tea and thin bread and butter with perhaps one sort of cake is offered in winter, or water ice in summer with wafers, there is nothing to be said against such a mode of hospitality, but if there is to be a variety of cakes, confectioneries, etc., anything that involves much expense or time, the " five o'clock tea " loses its original character and becomes a formal reception.

To have five o'clock tea weekly, if we have a number of friends dropping in, is a kindly and gracious custom. The tea is always made by the lady on the table and handed by her to her guests if there are no gentlemen to carry it (a servant should not be employed in the matter), the tea equipage consisting of a tray covered with a pretty cloth, with small cups and saucers, cream, sugar, slop bowl, the teapot covered with a cosey, and very thin bread and butter on plates. The tray is set on a table and the tea made. This is the English fashion. You may however prefer to use a table on which is the cloth without a tray; in this case the tea is not brought in but arranged ready for callers. Tea is made by the lady in the following way: The tea-pot has a little hot water in it when brought in; this must be poured out into the slop bowl and tea put in it according to the number you may require it for; three teaspoonfuls make a pint of tea, the cups used run three to the half pint. A quart of tea therefore will serve eight or nine, and allow for a second cup, which is rarely asked for. Of course, you must gauge your tea-pot, know how much it holds, and pour the water accordingly. When you put the tea in the pot light the alcohol kettle which should have had boiling water in it, and when it boils pour on to the tea about a third of the water you intend to use, put the cosey over it and let it steep seven minutes, add the rest of the water, cover again and use as needed; or, you may if you prefer, pour on all the water at once. It is easier and less formal to say to each guest after a few minutes' conversation, " Shall I give you some tea ? " or its equivalent, and to give it at once, than to wait to a certain time and hand it to every one at once. With the tea cosey the tea keeps hot a long time, but if people straggle in, or for any late comer, fresh should be made. A friendly, nice way, is to have a bright kettle on an open fire and make tea from that when boiling, in the good old-fashioned way. ·

CHAPTER XV.

I HAD chiefly in mind in the last chapter a class of women who perhaps may form but a small minority of my readers, namely, those who have large households and easy means, but there are others who have large households simply because they have a large house, and must have the servants to keep it clean, but who nevertheless need to be very economical. To these and those who have to provide for boarders or large numbers in any way, I would suggest the buying of many things in large quantities as a much better way of economizing than cutting down supplies or buying inferior ones. Butter may be bought by the pail in October, generally at 25 cents a pound, eggs in September are 20 cents or less, cases of assorted canned goods are much cheaper than by the single can, and there are many other things which it will be well worth while for those who need to be economical to inquire about. Of course, if you buy in bulk you will have to watch the consumption ; it is quite a common thing to hear the mistress of a house say, "I like to buy in large quantities, but if I get a pail of butter it goes like magic, and a barrel of apples lasts no longer than half a bushel." Of course, a barrel of apples open to every passing hand will go if it is not in the store-room ; they will be eaten, not because they are needed, but just "for fun ;" and as apples always seem free plunder, two or three will go out of the house in every pocket perhaps, without any idea of pilfering. Such stores should be under your own charge, or that of some one deputed by you, and given as required for use ; the butter also. With regard to butter, to keep it sweet, it requires such care that you will do well, aside from being able to know how it is used, to allow no one to handle it but yourself or your deputy ; if left uncovered or taken out with a soiled or warm spoon or ladle, it will be injured. Eggs may be preserved for winter use, either in lime water or in common dry salt, and be as fresh as those for which you will pay 35 to 40 cents the dozen at Christmas.

If you have a cool cellar or outhouse, you will do well in winter to buy half a sheep at a time, or even a whole one ; there is a good deal of fat on it, but it is valuable. You will not pay for the whole sheep more than twelve cents a pound and the waste is very small. The head, well cleaned, makes excellent broth; the scrag, although few people know it, is the most tender and finely flavored part for boiling, although it does not make a sightly dish ; it should be gently boiled twenty minutes to each pound, with a turnip, carrot and onion in the water, and a scant teaspoonful of salt to each quart ; the water only just to cover the meat. Serve it smothered in parsley or caper sauce. The broth may have the yolks of two eggs and a teaspoonful of finely chopped parsley beaten into it just before serving, or a little rice or pearl barley may have been boiled in it with the meat. Mutton broth prepared thus is delicious.

This part of mutton, too, makes that excellent Scotch dish, hotch-potch. The breast is the least manageable part of the animal, and yet two or three excellent dishes can be made from it ; if you will put it in water and let it boil slowly so as to extract the greater part of the fat, what will remain after three hours simmering will be marrowy and delicious; the bones may then be slipped out and a veal or other forcemeat laid in it, then rolled and roasted, or it may be made into excellent curry. All the fat should be saved and tried out ; keep one nice large jar of the finest for seething and pouring hot over preserves, potted meats, etc. The rest will make excellent hard soap.

It is needless to say, I suppose, that the longer mutton is hung in cold weather, the finer it is. If you have any man about you who understands cutting up meat, it is well to leave it hanging whole in a current of pure air, but otherwise pay a butcher's man a trifle to cut it up for you and then *hang* the parts ; remember, the head, neck, and forequarter, generally keep less well than the hindquarter. Wherever the meat has been cut, dredge flour until it forms a dry covering ; remove the pith from the whole length of the back bone. If a thaw comes on suddenly, and a warm spell sets in while you have much on hand, it is unfortunate, but the meat can be saved ; it is well, however, to avoid purchasing largely after long-continued frost. Of course, the usual winter thaws which last for a day or so, will not affect your meat much, but it is well to examine it, without bringing it into a warm temperature. If it is oozing at any spot, yet smells sweet, simply dredge more flour. If you fear that it is in danger, make the fat you have tried out boiling hot in some large vessel, a deep milk pan will do, then seethe the joints in this fat for a minute or two, one at a time, take each out, do not lay it down, but hang it quickly, just as it is, in a cold place ; the fat will chill on it and form a sort of air proof casing, which can be scraped off when required for use. Some parts, such as have many crevices, may be better half cooked, but for the legs, hind loin, or any solid compact meat, in fact, this is far the better method.

Meat that has hung long must be carefully scraped and washed off with vinegar and water, as the outer skin will have acquired a stale taste. I have known. an epicure to keep legs of mutton two months by care and watching, and at the end of the time the outer skin would be covered with blue mould ; this was skinned off as thin as possible, then the leg dredged with flour and roasted, and certainly it was tender as meat could possibly be, and the flavor very fine. In buying mutton for economy, do not choose it too fat, and give the preference to that with the smallest shank bone.

Beef bills will also be much cheaper if the beef is bought by the quarter. The hindquarter usually costs from 13 cents to 14 cents per pound ; the forequarter several cents less; although in the forequarter there are some good steaks and a few pounds of fair roast, it is more fit for families where a la mode beef, stewed beef, and much soup is required. For this reason it may be profitably bought for large boarding-houses which consume a great deal of meat for these purposes; but private families will do better to pay a little more for the hindquarter; all the best cuts are in this, and what are not required for roasts and steaks can be corned; the leg will be used for soup, and the fat (not suet) tried out for dripping, which is the next best thing to butter for all cooking purposes. The suet may be freed from skin and veins, chopped very fine and put into paper bags with a little dry flour. It will keep months in a dry cool place.

CHAPTER XVI.

WITH the fast approaching spring days will come a change in our way of living. If we are wise, on warm "Spring feverish" days we shall abandon a part of our strong meat diet and substitute vegetables—cereals, eggs, salads and fruits when they come. If city people who have bought meat for breakfast during winter, and feel they cannot afford cream, would drop the meat and take cream in its stead, using it with oatmeal, hominy or mush, they would be quite as well nourished, and better prepared to meet the warm languid days which spring often brings us.

The foregoing paragraph, however, has been written rather as a reminder of the changes that nature requires than because I intend to enter into dietetic matters. Before us lies the necessary but uninteresting matter of housecleaning.

There are very good housekeepers who say they have no housecleaning, that the house should be always clean. That is quite true, but, unless you are very severe to yourself and are quite certain you never store away what is useless, that you have the time, if you do your own work, the faithful service, if you do not to clean every nook and corner, I think the twice-yearly housecleaning is a good thing. There is one housekeeper I know of, who prides herself on never having a housecleaning time, but I think even those who groan in spirit over the semi-annual upturnings, would not envy this family, for the housecleaning is going on more or less all the time.   She says she takes up carpets when they require it; I do not believe it is oftener than twice a year, but it always seems that one or another room is in a dismantled condition. I know of others who deprecate housecleaning because life is not long enough to worry over it.   If things are really not dirty, what matter if the dust has accumulated in remote corners, it is only dust, innocuous, odorless dust.   Suppose the carpet swept weekly with tea leaves from year's end to year's end should have a thick layer of it underneath, and is going to wear out in less time, this philosophical housewife— no, housewife is not the term, philosopher is better, said, "reckon the two or three dollars a year it costs to shake it, the wear and tear of the process, and I don't believe I lose more than that by leaving it down three years."   Now, this family were cultivated people of refined habits, industrious, and by no means dirty, as might be expected, nor did their house present any appearance of neglect; on the contrary, I have known houses were dust was relentlessly pursued which were much less neat in appearance, but it did lack brightness and freshness, even abundant and beautiful flowers could not give that; nothing reflected a cheery light.   Do not many housekeepers know that before housecleaning begins nothing seems soiled?   One weary with many tasks may even ask if it can be necessary, and yet after it is over, she will see the difference ; the light will play on gleaming surfaces, the whole house seems brighter, more airy, and cheerful. Therefore, I say, let us have the housecleaning when possible, but let us not worry or fret if sickness at the season, or the pressure of other work or care makes it impossible. But when we clean house, let it be done with as little general discomfort as possible.

Closets may be emptied of contents one at a time on spring days before fires have quite ceased; all parcels, if parcels there be, opened, aired ; the contents, if we wish to keep them, may be repacked and labeled, the shelves washed down and sprinkled with powdered borax, and the packages replaced ; this will very much simplify the housecleaning when it comes. It often happens that garments we have put away to make over in fall, we may decide not to use but give them away. Apropos of old garments to be made over, it saves space and time to get them ready to begin work upon before packing away, and besides if a garment is put away soiled, just as you leave it off, it will look much worse when you take it out ; every spot and stain will show doubly, and the ripping be twice as disagreeable ; old housekeepers do not need to be told this, but inexperienced ones may. To such, I recommend that they rip, brush, sponge, and press all goods before laying away. They thus get rid of the dirt and dust, and parts too worn to be of service.

Perhaps a few directions for renovating certain articles may be of service to those about to put away winter things. Black silk may be sponged with a decoction of soap bark and water if very dirty, and hung out to dry, or if only creased and needing to be freshened, weak borax water or alcohol, and where possible, it is better pressed by laying pieces smoothly and pressing them through the clothes wringer screwed very tight.   If you must iron, do it after the silk is dry, between two damp pieces of muslin ; the upper one may better be Swiss, that you may see what you are doing through it.   This is a little more trouble than ironing the wrong side of silk, but you will be repaid ; the hot iron gives the silk a paper-like feeling ; above all, never iron silk wet, or even very damp.

Satin may be cleaned by sponging *lengthwise*—never across the width—with benzine, if greasy, or alcohol, or borax water ; this will not be injured by direct contact with iron ; press on the wrong side.   Black cloth may be sponged with ammonia and water, an ounce of rock ammonia to a wine bottle of water, or liquid household ammonia, diluted very much, may be used. Black cashmere may be washed in borax water, and so indeed, may navy blue.   It should be rubbed only between the hands, not on a board, and the water only pressed, *not twisted* out; each width folded in four as smoothly as possible, and wrung through the wringer, then opened and hung up to dry is the best way.   Cashmere so treated, if it is good quality, will look like new.

Pongee silk is supposed by many never to look so well after washing; but if properly treated, it may be made up again with new added, and the difference cannot be seen.   But as usually washed, it is several shades darker, and sometimes has a stiffness to it, although it may not have been starched; this change of color and stiffness is due to its being ironed wet. Again a pongee dress will come from the laundress covered with dark spots ; this is where it has been allowed to dry and then been " sprinkled down ;" the sprinkling shows. The remedy is simply to put it again in water, dry it and iron it when quite dry. Pongee requires no more care in washing than a white garment ; it will bear hard rubbing if necessary, but it must not be boiled or scalded. Treat it about as you would flannel; let it get *quite* dry, and if you use a quite hot iron, not hot enough to singe of course, all the creases will come out, and the silk will look like new. The reason it darkens it to iron it wet, is this : If it were put into boiling water the silk would darken as flannel would. If you put a hot iron on the damp silk you convert what water remains in it into boiling water; it is thus scalded. A silk which has changed color in the wash may be partly restored by washing again. Parenthetically, I may remark that this ironing them wet is the reason gentlemen's white silk handkerchiefs become yellow with washing.

While looking over the linen closet preparatory to housecleaning, notice what sheets are wearing thin in the middle and require turning. When *cotton* sheets become so it is hardly worth while in these days of precious time and cheap muslin to turn them. It is better to lay aside those that will not stand much more washing and keep them for sickness or times when frequent changes are required. This is a better way than to reserve strong new sheets for occasional use, and wear the old ones to rags. After closets, bureau drawers may have the same leisurely going over instead of leaving them until housecleaning is in full career. If this is done, and only one room thoroughly cleaned at a time, housecleaning need not be the terror it is. It may take two weeks instead of one if you have ten or twelve rooms, and only try to get one done in a short day, which is usually easy enough to do if there are two working. Although we know there are many women who do work entirely alone, it is very hard, indeed, for one woman to take down bedsteads and shake carpets, and move heavy furniture, not to speak of taking down and moving stoves; yet, I have known women do all this and more, but to some it would be physically impossible, and many who do it ought not to do it; they may suffer all the latter part of their lives from abuse of the inexhaustible energy which leads them to overtax themselves. To women so situated and so constituted, I would give the advice which I fear they will not, perhaps cannot, follow. Cultivate a wholesome habit of negligence, it is better the stove remain up all summer if heavy than you should move it; better a dusty carpet for a few months than that you should lay up for yourself an early old age. Not that housework, scrubbing, cleaning, even beyond what is looked upon as a woman's limit is hurtful, if not carried beyond your strength; if you can trust yourself to cease when you are really and heartily tired, when rest is refreshment; but too many women work just to finish this or that, long after fatigue has set in. Their bodies may not feel much more tired than they were an hour or two earlier, but instead of cheerful physical fatigue, when it is real comfort to sit down and rest, and laugh and talk perhaps, or read something pleasant ; instead of this good feeling, has come nervous fatigue, a very different matter, the least word irritates us, and when we finally cease, it is not to rest with cheerful talk or reading and a delicious sense of work done and repose earned, but we sink down too tired to rest, feeling worn out, ill, and ready to cry rather than laugh. We may get over once, such abuse as this, or two or three times, but by degrees this nervous irritability will become, not a rare experience consequent on rare fatigue, but will follow even very little exertion, and the result will be, the shattered, pallid woman faded and worn out long before life's prime, and probably the time will then have come for her, when she not only is not able to do very much, but she is unable to refrain from trying to do. Therefore, I say, if the work that seems so necessary causes more than a healthy fatigue, let it go. Keep the house " broom clean ; " do just what *must* be done and reserve your nerves for your husband and children ; it is your duty. If you do your own washing, since cleanliness is next to godliness, and it *must* be done, use every labor-saving article within your reach ; iron only the necessary. Use the wringer as a mangle ; when sheets and towels and undergarments are dry and smoothly folded, run them through the wringer instead of ironing them ; they will be just as wholesome and your back will be saved.

I repeat, this advice is only to the over-burdened; to the strong, energetic woman whose washing, ironing and churning leave her, only muscle weary, but full of vitality and ready to welcome fresh work next day, I can only say "good speed." Your work benefits you, as a course of athletics would. The youngest woman of her age that I know, pretty and bright, and full of the enjoyment of life in spite of several grand-children, tells me she had six children, no servant till they were all out of hand, and she did her own white-washing, painting and wall papering, but she was never unwise enough to work in a hurry; she had much to do, but she did not worry to do it all in a given time; and then again, although she is a small woman, she must have enjoyed perfect health and an equable temperament.

Now that I have said enough I hope, to show my readers that I do not look upon it as *every* woman's duty to do all the work I shall indicate for house-cleaning; I shall proceed to tell what—when there are hands to do it—is advisable to have done once or twice a year. That plan of housecleaning is best, I think, which begins with the bedrooms, getting, un-less there is an unusual reason for not doing it, one room furnished and comfortable, before another is upset, then coming down to the lower rooms, and then the garret, kitchen and cellar last of all. My reason for putting the garret or lumber room after lower rooms, is because in the process of turning out and cleaning below, many things may be relegated to the garret, and if it has already been gone over, there will needs be some time again spent there to arrange the fresh consignments. I will say here what I have to suggest about the garret, because in spite of my own view, many will cling to the old practice and prefer to go literally from "garret to cellar."

The most difficult part, I think, in the tidying of the garret, is not the cleaning; that I will not enter into as the directions given for bedrooms can be modified to suit the garrets. Some are simply unfinished lumber rooms, and all you can do is to sweep the dust and cobwebs off the walls and floor and then mop the latter. Other garrets are to all intents and purposes excellent rooms, and will be cleaned as such. No, the true difficulty is in arranging the articles stored in the garret so that they can be immediately found. The first thing I would counsel, is to get rid of articles you do not need; all pieces of worn out garments, anything that we may not have been sure about last cleaning, but now we know we shall never use; put these things from the piece bag to the rag bag, which can be emptied the first time the junkman comes round; in going over trunks every parcel should be opened, contents noted, marked in pencil (or still better, with a "stylo," for ink will not rub) on a slip of paper and fastened to it. How much time this labeling saves, every woman can tell who has hunted through a dozen parcels to find a piece of silk or velvet, she well knows is with some package of pieces. Many classify articles stowed away, as all colored woolens in one parcel tied with a piece of the goods to indicate contents; all black woolens another package, one of silks, etc.; but so many things defy us to class them, they seem to belong nowhere, and we would gladly get rid of them, but are sure we should some day, for ourselves or others, be glad to run to the garret and get them.

A great assistance is a large wall bag which to a housekeeper, is what a desk full of pigeon-holes is to the business man. I will describe this "housekeeper's friend" for those who may not have seen one. It is a large piece of strong gray drilling with a dozen (or more or less) pockets sewed on, three rows of four pockets, or four rows of three according as you have a long or broad wall space on which to hang it. These pockets are from six inches deep and five broad to twelve by ten, according to the stowing room you require. They are stitched on and on each is written in large plain letters with ink the contents; for instance buttons, tapes, ribbons, braids, curtain rings, etc.; in short, all the articles that may be too useful to throw away, yet because they are not new or seldom used, may not find a place in the work basket. Ribbons a little soiled, just the thing to line or bind or strengthen some article, tapes still strong, or buttons from a garment old-fashioned but sure to come in again, odd buttons too, that only encumber the regular button box. All the odds and ends we may think it a sort of a duty to keep, if we have a thrifty soul, yet which are a nuisance if we constantly come across them, may find appropriate homes in these bags. When all boxes, packages, etc., have been gone over, the cleaning may be done according to the kind of room the garret is, the one thing necessary always being, that it shall be made free from dust, and so far as possible the danger of insect breeding lessened.

In what I am about to say of spring cleaning, it will be remembered that I mean turning out one room at a time, and getting everything back in its place before another is displaced ; when the closets and bureaus are already clean this is very quickly done, (unless your bedstead requires special attention, which I hope may not be the case.) It is not the actual cleaning that takes long, but the small preparations for it. The first step is to get rid of the stove, take away the ashes, beat the soot out of the pipes and stow away in a dry place till fall ; then, if you have a piazza roof or other convenience, put the mattress out of the window to air and to be beaten ; if not, put it wherever you may have space. Take off the spring, examine it thoroughly, dust every part, (an old tooth brush or duck wing will go into crevices), put this out of the room ; then take the bedstead down. If you are free from parasites, dust every crevice and put the different parts outside the room door. If you are not free from bed-bugs, and there may be circumstances which will make it difficult to keep free, you need to pay special attention to your bedstead. Sometimes during a summer, bed-bugs are brought into the house by visitors, travelers, etc., and when one remembers that one female is enough to populate a room, and that some houses so swarm with them that they are on the clothes of all who leave it, it is far more remarkable that we escape the infliction than that we have it, considering how many people of all kinds we jostle in our out-door life.

If then you have been unfortunate enough to have had bed-bugs brought to you, of which you hope you are rid, nevertheless, it will be well to act as if something might certainly be lurking in some crevice invisible to your eye. Provide yourself with a cent's worth of white lead and some sublimate of mercury (or in default of that, some strong yellow soap and kerosene), a feather, and a machine oil can or glass syringe; dip the feather in the sublimate, insert it in *every* crevice, brush over all larger surfaces, such as ends of the slats, places where they rest, etc.; put into the oil can, or syringe, a little of the sublimate, and inject it into all worm-holes or cavities where eggs may have been deposited, then with the white lead and an old knife, fill up every accidental crack or crevice, remembering the loathsome insect loves to deposit eggs in cracks of the slat, in the crevices around knots, and where splinters have broken off. If your white lead is hard, moisten with oil, then plug up holes, cracks, abrasions, worm-holes, and make smooth surfaces with it, wherever the wood is rough. It will spread like putty. (Use soap just in the same way, and the kerosene as you do the sublimate.) In fact, it is better not to wait for the appearance of vermin to do this, but to go over a new bedstead in the same way, especially if it is an expensive one. If you do not like the appearance of such white filling, any paint store where you buy the white lead will color it to match the wood. Persian insect powder is harm-

less and excellent, but not so powerful as the sublimate. Even if you should find traces in your bedstead
of the presence of the enemy, but to no great extent,
these precautions, applied, of course, just as thoroughly
to the spring mattress, will suffice to rid you of them,
but for months it will be well to take off the spring
every week, remove the slats and carefully examine
the bedstead. If, however, you are unfortunate
enough to have your rooms infested or even your bedstead, and you wish to be permanently rid of them,
you must take much stronger measures ; and as such
a task would necessitate two or three days' work, I
will not just here interrupt the housecleaning proceed-
ings to describe it, but will return to the subject later.

When the bedstead has been put outside, draw
tacks, take up the carpet and put it in the yard or
wherever it is to be beaten. Throw wet paper, tea
leaves or sawdust on the floor and then sweep it ;
brush off the skirting board, tops of doors and windows, and then brush down the walls. If the paper
is handsome and of fine quality and there are grease
spots, it may be cleaned by laying over them a paste
made of magnesia and benzine. A shabby paper may
also be improved by rubbing with stale bread, although
I think I should prefer, as an easier task, to paper
the room afresh with some low-priced, artistic paper.
It is a good plan once a year to go round each room
and hall, and, wherever paper has been jagged or dis-
figured, lay little pieces on it matching the pattern exactly. For small surfaces the mucilage bottle is all
that is required to make the repairs. When the dam-

age is more serious, paste may be made for the purpose in the following way : Mix one tablespoonful of flour with a *little* cold water, pour to it half a pint of boiling water, stirring as you pour,—in fact just make it as you would starch, then boil two or three minutes. The task of repairing paper, however, had better be done before the cleaning day. On that day you want to have as little hindrance as possible from small things.

When the dust is all removed clean the paint. In doing this, if it is white or very light, use only a wet flannel smeared with whitening—no soap ; otherwise use good soap, and change the water very often ; clean up and down as the painter's brush has gone, wash off the soapy lather with the flannel wrung through the water, then *wipe with a dry cloth.* Wiping dry and using clean water will prevent the smeary look that is sometimes seen on paint.

In washing the floor use strong borax water, and if you have buffalo moths sprinkle the floor freely with powdered borax or powdered alum. As all bedrooms require about the same process, and dining and drawing rooms differ only in having cabinets or sideboard to be thoroughly cleaned instead of the bedstead, I will not repeat processes, but speak of matters which, although not necessarily belonging to housecleaning yet as the cleaning is often the season for changing the appearance of rooms, will come in appropriately.

After the winter's wear, hard-wood floors look much better for a coat of shellac varnish, "or hard oil finish" applied with a soft varnish brush. This can easily be done by any lady herself at the expense of a back ache, but the economy of doing this one's self is considerable, and the work is well repaid by the result. A large carpet worn shabby in parts will often make an excellent rug; if the floor is well stained, the room will have a better appearance than when fully carpeted. I have spoken of preparing a floor staining, in a former chapter, and if for a parlor,—unless the pine floor is much better laid than usual,—the carpenter's services to smooth off and fill in the spaces will be necessary; but bed-rooms may be easily stained by any amateur, and, unless cracks are very wide, the filling may be dispensed with. I prefer for stain to buy a box of burnt umber (30 cents) and a quart or two quarts of turpentine, to purchasing the prepared stains. It is a little cheaper, for one reason, but my chief one is that the prepared stain is often very black. I think the stain is prettier if the grain of the pine shows through it, and for it to do this the stain must be very thin, not darker than black walnut.

You require a broad brush, an old tin can of small size, or gallipot not very deep, and a piece of board— the lid of a starch box will do, it is only to try the color. Now open the umber, take out a small quantity with your brush—it is a thick, blackish paste— put in this vessel you have provided and pour turpentine on it, a little at a time, stirring and trying the color till you have it right. (It is better too light than too dark. The last shows dust and does not imitate any wood in use for hard floors.) You had better not mix more than a pint or less at a time, as the turpentine evaporates so fast ; and each time you mix be sure you get about the color of the first.   If by chance or imperfect mixing one spot is darker than the other, go over it before it dries with clear turpentine.   The stain dries quickly, but you had better paint yourself out of the room and not tread on it for a few hours.

It is sometimes recommended simply to oil the surface after staining and to wash with oil and water, but this is a great mistake ; it will look well for a time, but the pine is so absorbent that the oil sinks in and soon becomes gummy.   At this stage no amount of washing will make it look clean ; the dirt sticks to the old oil, and there is nothing to do but cover the floor up or have it planed.   If after staining you go over it with a coat of shellac varnish, this will fill up the pores of the wood so that none of the cleaning oil or water will be absorbed.   Oil will not be needed in the water for a long time if the water it is washed with is always clear, and the floor is well swept before the washing is done.

The foregoing is the simplest kind of staining, but a much better effect may be produced by having a border.   This may be one or two bands of light oak. To do this draw lines with a carpenter's pencil, on the floor, round the room.   An easy way is to lay a bed-slat on the floor about four inches from the skirting board and draw a line each side of it.   The width is just about right for the band.   Of course you go round the room with it.   If you want a second band, leave a space an inch or so wider than the slat and mark as before. If measuring and marking by a carpenter's rule seems easier than the slat, do it that way. At the corners of the room you may lay your rule or slat diagonally from band to band, or, have any parquet design you please.

You will use the dark stain for the strip between the skirting board and the first penciled line. Be very careful not to go over it; if you should do so, wipe off the stain with a rag and turpentine, then stain dark the space between the two penciled bands, then the center of the room. When the dark stain *is dry*, stain the bands and corner designs with light oak stain, which can be bought by that name. Be very careful to keep within the lines, for the sharper these bands are defined, the better your work. If you have an accident and encroach on the dark stain, you can wash it off with turpentine, but this will leave a blurred appearance. The shellac varnish must be applied over all when dry. In using shellac, work quickly, as it hardens rapidly, and if slowly done the coat may be uneven.

The servant's room will require your personal attention before the bedroom cleaning is done, and if you suspect it to contain vermin, I advise it to be the first room cleaned, for obvious reasons. It seems rather hard that one should have to give personal attention to the servant's bedstead, but in self-defense it is imperative. She may be excellent and cleanly in all ways, yet in the homes of her friends, the lodgings she uses when out of place, bed-bugs swarm.

You will tell her to examine her bedstead, and she will do so to the best of her ability; but unless they have been more neglected than is probable with any reader of these papers, that is, unless bed-bugs are visible in corners of the mattress and on the ends of slats, she will certainly not see them. The fact is she does not know *how to look;* she does not dream of probing and searching, so when she has removed a few slats and found nothing, she thinks further search useless; or she may tell you: "There was *hardly* anything, but I gave the bedstead a good washing," etc., etc.

If you are fortunate enough to have old, tried and experienced servants, you may be able to spare yourself the disgusting task which so many ladies have to perform, not once but many times,—a task all the more disagreeable if the servant is of the better, self-respecting kind, and whose privacy we are able and anxious to respect; I take it that no well-bred woman likes to intrude in her servant's bedroom, unless she finds she cannot be trusted to keep it clean.

As I wish here to give some directions for thoroughly cleansing an infested room, I will assume that the servant's bedstead requires strong measures, and, if that is the case, the walls require attention too. Let me say here that this task no housekeeper can avoid doing personally except at the expense of the whole house being troubled, unless she employs a man who makes such business a specialty. Most painters will know of one.

Of course you will not have paper on the walls of the room; hard finish is best. This should be examined, and every crack and crevice or nail hole filled up with plaster of Paris mixed to paste with water. It hardens almost at once, so do not mix until about to use. All round the skirting board should be injected with kerosene; wherever there are crevices near the bed, these filled with plaster of Paris. This filling up all openings, however small, I advise even in a room that is quite free from the pest. Prevention is better than cure. In a room where they are established in the walls, it is well to fumigate. As the first step after the bedstead has been taken down, thoroughly searched in all unlikely, as well as likely, places, the casters being laid in kerosene, and the holes where they belong being injected with sublimate, inject the same far into every hole and socket, then go over all corners, ends of laths, etc., with a hard brush, dipped in sublimate. Corners of the mattress, tufting, etc., all must be treated with the sublimate; and then stuff up windows and keyholes, hang up a heavy blanket outside the door, securely fasten with two kitchen forks or nails, and then, removing from the room looking-glass and any metal articles there may be, leave bedding, etc., to be fumigated. The easiest way is to use a charcoal furnace, but if you put two bricks on the floor, a coal-hod or old tin pan can be set on with live coals. Have in your hand a packet of powdered sulphur; stand ready to close the door of the room instantly; then from the doorway throw the paper packet on to the coals, close the door drop the blanket and set a chair to keep the blanket close so as to confine the fumes. Next day hold your breath, when you enter the room, till you have thrown open the window. The contents of the room should now go into the open air.

This fumigation is necessary for any room where the trouble is deep-seated. In giving these directions I am supposing an extreme case, but in what I am now going to say about the bedstead, I give my own plan, whether the trouble is present or not. In many years' housekeeping I have had real trouble but once, and I think the reason is the precaution I take. Every fall, after examining the servant's bedstead, I paint the ends of the slats, the places where they rest, the bed spring, every bit of the woodwork, on which the mattress rests, with thin white paint in which there is a good deal of turpentine.

In changing servants, I never let a new one come into the room as left by the last, but make a thorough examination of bed and bedstead, and use the paint brush, unless recently done.

I believe hard, white varnish, used instead of paint, is even better, but the latter is cheap and easy, and I have found effectual. The chief thing is, it fills up the pores of the wood and makes rough places smoother, and no longer suitable depositing places for eggs. The ends of slats in cheap bedsteads are often very coarsely sawn off, and these pores are often full of eggs, which are nearly invisible. Paint cures all this. But you may do all this and more, and yet if you leave such a bedstead in such a room unvisited till next cleaning time, you will probably again find the pest; some one of them, somewhere, will have escaped and undone your work, therefore for weeks look every day or two to see that no chance be given to their unfortunate fecundity.

A handsome bedstead you would not like to treat with paint, and if you have one that has been troubled, after thorough cleansing with the sublimate, sprinkle plentifully with genuine insect powder, and after that, every morning for months, devote half an hour to a thorough examination of the bed. Once a week take it down. With this treatment, once thorough cleaning, then *daily* inspection, you will effectually rid yourself of the pests, even if they were very bad. Too often the thorough cleansing is done, then the matter given up for several weeks or months, but then surely it must all be gone over again, and so on for years, and one is never free. I confess, in the bright spring and summer mornings, it is hard to give up half an hour to such a task, especially when day after day we find nothing to justify the search, but it is only for a time, and it is only by such ceaseless following up that you can be sure of getting free from what is a perpetual dread and horror, so long as it lasts.

All else that concerns housekeeping has, I think, been gone into in the methods of work given for each day. It only remains for me to say, with regard to the household work, that the work of summer differs very little from winter, except that the fires are done away with, and, instead of having ashes to remove, and ventilation to manage without letting too much frosty air into the house, we can throw open windows and let in floods of sunshine and fresh air, while the outside porches or stoops are brushed or washed.

I have been asked two or three questions, which I take this opportunity of answering. One is in relation to dish-*towels;* the other, to dish-*cloths,* often called dish-*rags.* This should never be an appropriate term, for while one might, for want of better, take a rag to dust with, a rag should not serve for dishes, but a decent cloth. Old *crash* dish-towels have usually strong ends which can be cut off and *hemmed,* and a loop put into it, for a dish-cloth. But a yard of coarse, strong, twilled dish-toweling can be cut in three, and hemmed and looped. This is the better way, for you can find excellent use for the old crash towels for drying cloths for floor or paint. I prefer to keep two dish-cloths in use,—one to be washed and dried each day. They will last twice as long as when allowed to be constantly wet. The most delightful dish-cloths are made of a ball of candle wick knitted on coarse, wooden needles, and, if dried each day, they wear very well. Do not allow dilapidated dish-cloths to be used; the lint is constantly passing into your waste-pipe, with the danger of stopping it up; and they are not easy to wash and dry. With regard to dish-towels, I think there is only one thing indispensable,—they must be of linen,—cotton loses color, and stains are difficult to wash out. The soft Russian crash is, I think, best, but some kinds are so hard it takes months to "break" them. Softer and finer linen toweling comes for glass and silver. It should be a rule to have them washed immediately after they have been used, and once a week they should be boiled and ironed, to keep them soft. If you happen to have the hard crash, have each towel ironed *every time* it is washed for a few weeks; this will rapidly soften it.

A lady has told me her method of taking up ashes, which seems so good that I give my readers the benefit of it. It is to lay a sheet of newspaper in the coal-hod, one page of it hanging over the sides. As each shovelful of ashes is put into the hod turn the loose leaf of paper over it while you take up the next shovelful. This prevents very much dust from rising.

I have said nothing at all on one subject, which belongs very intimately to housekeeping, yet I venture to think is not of it, any more than our courtship and marriage or other matters sacred to the inner life. I allude to children, but so serious, so many-sided is the subject of children's training, that it could not be effectively discussed in the scope of one of these chapters; and we may be sure the wife who keeps house well for her husband will do the same for the dear little ones. The judicious rules that make comfort in the house for one, make it for the whole family.

I wish to state here that there are several manufactured articles for cleaning purposes, of whose merits as labor-saving mediums I am well aware, and very heartily recommend all housekeepers to take advantage of them. The really valuable articles of this class have stood the test of time, and are so well known as to need no mention, but improvements on old methods are always taking place, and while it is unwise, if you have an article in use that completely answers its purpose, to displace it in favor of a newer kind, perhaps less good in reality, it is good to welcome any article which fills a long-felt want.

SUMMER PROGRAMME OF WORK.

General order of work for every day of summer:

Before leaving your room, throw open windows, top and bottom; lay pillows in the sun, bedclothes to air, and turn back mattress.

As soon as you come down stairs, open blinds and windows.

Light kitchen fire ; take up ashes; sift them.

Brush off the stove; rinse and fill the kettle.

Sweep the kitchen, the stoop or piazzas, beating all mats thoroughly.

Remove stale flowers from parlor and dining-room, and dust.

Prepare for breakfast, putting biscuit or muffins to bake, while you lay the table. Close blinds on the sunny side.

After breakfast, clear the table as soon as possible, putting milk and butter away at once, instead of allowing them to remain in the hot kitchen.

Do not leave the white table-cloth on a moment longer than necessary, as it attracts flies. For the same reason remove the crumbs from the floor. This applies to every meal.

Wash and put away breakfast dishes.

Darken the dining-room, pantry and all unused rooms.

Make beds, empty slops, wash soap-dishes, fill water pitchers, fold dry towels, take away soiled ones,—but if damp, dry them before putting into the soiled clothes-hamper, as everything quickly mildews in hot weather.

Darken rooms after having put them in perfect order.

Either now or before going up stairs, attend to the refrigerator—empty the drip-pan; remove everything that will not keep; wipe out sides and shelves with a large, coarse sponge kept for the purpose. If milk or other article has been spilt in it, wash it out with hot water and soda or borax. Keep pieces of charcoal in it, which change often, and occasionally, if it cannot be aired without danger of food spoiling, put a plate of *unslacked* lime in each compartment and leave it till it crumbles; this dries the air.

Then proceed to the special work for the day. (See programmes of special work in former chapters.)

If you are troubled with flies, the *last thing* before retiring, when all windows and doors are closed, puff Persian insect powder in the air of each room, closing the door after. Next morning, if the powder has been genuine (there is no article more adulterated, druggists tell me), you will find the place strewn with the slain, and a dusty deposit everywhere. This dust is the only objection to the use of powder, but it makes no more work than the flies themselves if they are unmolested, and is infinitely cleaner than plates of fly poison. The powder is simply the Persian camomile, not at all poisonous except to insect life; it may make you sneeze or cough a moment, as would flour or any other dust if the air were filled with it.

Burn or bury the flies you gather. It is said (but I have not tested the matter) that they are only stupefied and that after a day or so they come to life again. I do know, if this be so, that it takes many hours to restore them.

Works of fiction

PUBLISHED BY

HOUGHTON, MIFFLIN AND COMPANY,

4 Park St., Boston; 11 E. 17th St., New York.

———◆———

Thomas Bailey Aldrich.

Story of a Bad Boy. Illustrated. 12mo $1.25
Marjorie Daw and Other People. 12mo 1.50
Marjorie Daw and Other Stories. Riverside Aldine
Series. 16mo 1.00
Prudence Palfrey. 12mo 1.50
The Queen of Sheba. 12mo 1.50
The Stillwater Tragedy. 12mo 1.50

Hans Christian Andersen.

Complete Works. In ten uniform volumes, crown 8vo.
A new and cheap Edition, in attractive binding.
The Improvisatore; or, Life in Italy 1.00
The Two Baronesses 1.00
O. T.; or, Life in Denmark 1.00
Only a Fiddler 1.00
In Spain and Portugal 1.00
A Poet's Bazaar 1.00
Pictures of Travel 1.00
The Story of my Life. With Portrait 1.00
Wonder Stories told for Children. Illustrated . . . 1.00
Stories and Tales. Illustrated 1.00
    The set 10.00

B. B. B. Series.

Story of a Bad Boy. By T. B. Aldrich.
Captains of Industry. By James Parton.
Being a Boy. By C. D. Warner.
    The set, 3 vols. 16mo 3.75

William Henry Bishop.

Detmold: A Romance. "Little Classic" style. 18mo 1.25
The House of a Merchant Prince. 12mo 1.50
Choy Susan, and Other Stories. 16mo 1.25
The Golden Justice. 16mo. 1.25

Björnstjerne Björnson.

Works. *American Edition*, sanctioned by the author,
    and translated by Professor R. B. Anderson, of the
    University of Wisconsin.
Complete Works, in three volumes. 12mo. The set 4.50

Alice Cary.

Pictures of Country Life. 12mo $1.50

John Esten Cooke.

My Lady Pokahontas. 16mo 1.25

James Fenimore Cooper.

Complete Works. New *Household Edition*, in attractive binding. With Introductions to many of the volumes by Susan Fenimore Cooper, and Illustrations. In thirty-two volumes, 16mo.

Precaution.	The Prairie.
The Spy.	Wept of Wish-ton-Wish.
The Pioneers.	The Water Witch.
The Pilot.	The Bravo.
Lionel Lincoln.	The Heidenmauer.
Last of the Mohicans.	The Headsman.
Red Rover.	The Monikins.
Homeward Bound.	Miles Wallingford.
Home as Found.	The Red Skins.
The Pathfinder.	The Chainbearer.
Mercedes of Castile.	Satanstoe.
The Deerslayer.	The Crater.
The Two Admirals.	Jack Tier.
Wing and Wing.	The Sea Lions.
Wyandotté.	Oak Openings.
Afloat and Ashore.	The Ways of the Hour.

(*Each volume sold separately.*)

Each volume 1.00
The set 32.00

New Fireside Edition. With forty-five original Illustrations. In sixteen volumes, 12mo. The set . . . 20.00

(*Sold only in sets.*)

Sea Tales. New *Household Edition*, containing Introductions by Susan Fenimore Cooper. Illustrated. First Series. Including —

The Pilot.	The Red Rover.
The Water Witch.	The Two Admirals.
Wing and Wing.	

Second Series. Including —

The Sea Lions.	Afloat and Ashore.
Jack Tier.	Miles Wallingford.
The Crater.	

Each set, 5 vols. 16mo 5.00

Leather-Stocking Tales. New *Household Edition*, containing Introductions by Susan Fenimore Cooper. Illustrated. In five volumes, 16mo.

The Deerslayer.   The Pioneers.
The Pathfinder.   The Prairie.
Last of the Mohicans.
    The set $5.00
Cooper Stories; being Narratives of Adventure selected from his Works. With Illustrations by F. O. C. Darley. In three volumes, 16mo, each 1.00

Charles Egbert Craddock.
In the Tennessee Mountains. 16mo 1.25
The Prophet of the Great Smoky Mountains. 16mo . 1.25
Down the Ravine. Illustrated. 16mo 1.00
In the Clouds. 16mo 1.25
The Story of Keedon Bluffs. 16mo 1.00
The Despot of Broomsedge Cove. 16mo 1.25

Thomas Frederick Crane.
Italian Popular Tales. Translated from the Italian. With Introduction and a Bibliography. 8vo . . . 2.50

F. Marion Crawford.
To Leeward. 16mo 1.25
A Roman Singer. 16mo 1.25
An American Politician. 16mo 1.25
Paul Patoff. Crown 8vo 1.50

Maria S. Cummins.
The Lamplighter. 12mo 1.00
El Fureidîs. 12mo 1.50
Mabel Vaughan. 12mo 1.50

Parke Danforth.
Not in the Prospectus. 16mo 1.25

Daniel De Foe.
Robinson Crusoe. Illustrated. 16mo 1.00

Margaret Deland.
John Ward, Preacher. 12mo 1.50

P. Deming.
Adirondack Stories. 18mo 75
Tompkins and Other Folks. 18mo 1.00

Thomas De Quincey.
Romances and Extravaganzas. 12mo 1.50
Narrative and Miscellaneous Papers. 12mo . . . 1.50

Charles Dickens.
Complete Works. *Illustrated Library Edition.* With Introductions by E. P. Whipple. Containing Illustrations by Cruikshank, Phiz, Seymour, Leech, Mac-

lise, and others, on steel, to which are added designs of Darley and Gilbert, in all over 550. In twenty-nine volumes, 12mo.

The Pickwick Papers, 2 vols.	Dombey and Son, 2 vols.
Nicholas Nickleby, 2 vols.	Pictures from Italy, and
Oliver Twist.	American Notes.
Old Curiosity Shop, and Re-printed Pieces, 2 vols.	Bleak House, 2 vols.
	Little Dorrit, 2 vols.
Barnaby Rudge, and Hard Times, 2 vols.	David Copperfield, 2 vols.
	A Tale of Two Cities.
Martin Chuzzlewit, 2 vols.	Great Expectations.
Our Mutual Friend, 2 vols.	Edwin Drood, Master
Uncommercial Traveller.	Humphrey's Clock, and
A Child's History of England, and Other Pieces.	Other Pieces.
	Sketches by Boz.
Christmas Books.	

Each volume $1.50
The set.   With Dickens Dictionary.   30 vols . . 45.00
Christmas Carol.   Illustrated.   8vo, full gilt 2.50
The Same.   32mo . . . . ·75
Christmas Books.   Illustrated.   12mo 2.00

Charlotte Dunning.

A Step Aside.   16mo 1.25

Edgar Fawcett.

A Hopeless Case.   "Little Classic" style.   18mo   .   1.25
A Gentleman of Leisure. "Little Classic" style. 18mo   1.00
An Ambitious Woman.   12mo 1.50

Fénelon.

Adventures of Telemachus.   12mo 2.25

Mrs. James A. Field.

High-Lights.   16mo 1.25

Harford Flemming.

A Carpet Knight.   16mo 1.25

Baron de la Motte Fouqué.

Undine, Sintram and his Companions, etc.   32mo . . ·75
Undine and Other Tales.   Illustrated.   16mo . . . 1.00

Johann Wolfgang von Goethe.

Wilhelm Meister.   Translated by Thomas Carlyle.
Portrait of Goethe.   In two volumes.   12mo . . . 3.00
The Tale and Favorite Poems.   32mo . . . . . . ·75

Oliver Goldsmith.

Vicar of Wakefield. *Handy-Volume Edition.* 24mo,
gilt top $1.00
The Same. "Riverside Classics." Illustrated. 16mo 1.00

Jeanie T. Gould (Mrs. Lincoln).

Marjorie's Quest. Illustrated. 12mo 1.50

The Guardians.

A Novel 1.25

Thomas Chandler Haliburton.

The Clockmaker; or, The Sayings and Doings of
Samuel Slick of Slickville. Illustrated. 16mo . 1.00

A. S. Hardy.

But Yet a Woman. 16mo 1.25
The Wind of Destiny. 16mo 1.25

Miriam Coles Harris.

Rutledge.   Richard Vandermarck.   St. Philips.
The Sutherlands.   A Perfect Adonis.   Missy.
Frank Warrington. Happy-Go-Lucky.   Phœbe.
Each volume, 16mo. 1.25
Louie's Last Term at St. Mary's. 16mo 1.00

Bret Harte.

The Luck of Roaring Camp, and Other Sketches. 16mo 1.25
The Luck of Roaring Camp, and Other Stories.
Riverside Aldine Series. 16mo 1.00
Tales of the Argonauts, and Other Stories. 16mo . 1.25
Thankful Blossom. "Little Classic" style. 18mo . 1.00
Two Men of Sandy Bar. A Play. 18mo 1.00
The Story of a Mine. 18mo 1.00
Drift from Two Shores. 18mo 1.00
Twins of Table Mountain, etc. 18mo 1.00
Flip, and Found at Blazing Star. 18mo 1.00
In the Carquinez Woods. 18mo 1.00
On the Frontier "Little Classic" style. 18mo . . 1.00
Works. Rearranged, with an Introduction and a
Portrait. In six volumes, crown 8vo.
Poetical Works, and the drama, "Two Men of Sandy
Bar," with an Introduction and Portrait.
The Luck of Roaring Camp, and Other Stories.
Tales of the Argonauts and Eastern Sketches.
Gabriel Conroy.
Stories and Condensed Novels.
Frontier Stories.
Each volume 2.00
The set 12.00

By Shore and Sedge. 18mo $1.00
Maruja. A Novel. 18mo 1.00
Snow-Bound at Eagle's. 18mo 1.00
The Queen of the Pirate Isle. A Story for Children.
    Illustrated by Kate Greenaway. Small 4to . . . 1.50
A Millionaire of Rough-and-Ready, and Devil's Ford.
    18mo 1.00
The Crusade of the Excelsior. Illustrated. 16mo . 1.25
A Phyllis of the Sierras, and A Drift from Redwood
    Camp. 18mo 1.00
The Argonauts of North Liberty. 18mo 1.00

Wilhelm Hauff.

Arabian Days Entertainments. Illustrated. 12mo . 1.50

Nathaniel Hawthorne.

Works. *New Riverside Edition.* With an original
    etching in each volume, and a new Portrait. With
    bibliographical notes by George P. Lathrop. Com-
    plete in twelve volumes, crown 8vo.
Twice-Told Tales.
Mosses from an Old Manse.
The House of the Seven Gables, and The Snow-Image.
The Wonder-Book, Tanglewood Tales, and Grand-
    father's Chair.
The Scarlet Letter, and The Blithedale Romance.
The Marble Faun.
Our Old Home, and English Note-Books. 2 vols.
American Note-Books.
French and Italian Note-Books.
The Dolliver Romance, Fanshawe, Septimius Felton,
    and, in an Appendix, the Ancestral Footstep.
Tales, Sketches, and Other Papers. With Biograph-
    ical Sketch by G. P. Lathrop, and Indexes.
        Each volume 2.00
        The set 24.00
New " *Little Classic* " *Edition.* Each volume contains
    Vignette Illustration. In twenty-five volumes, 18mo.
        Each volume 1.00
        The set 25.00
New *Wayside Edition.* With Portrait, twenty-three
    etchings, and Notes by George P. Lathrop. In
    twenty-four volumes, 12mo 36.00
New *Fireside Edition.* In six volumes, 12mo . . . 10.00
A Wonder-Book for Girls and Boys. *Holiday Edi-*
    tion. With Illustrations by F. S. Church. 4to . 2.50
The Same. 16mo, boards 40
Tanglewood Tales. With Illustrations by Geo.
    Wharton Edwards. 4to, full gilt 2.50

The Same. 16mo, boards $0.40
Twice-Told Tales. *School Edition.* 18mo 1.00
The Scarlet Letter. *Popular Edition.* 12mo . . . 1.00
True Stories from History and Biography. 12mo . 1.25
The Wonder-Book. 12mo 1.25
Tanglewood Tales. 12mo 1.25
The Snow-Image. Illustrated in colors. Small 4to . .75
Grandfather's Chair. *Popular Edition.* 16mo, paper
    covers 15
Tales of the White Hills, and Legends of New Eng-
    land. 32mo 75
Legends of Province House, and A Virtuoso's Col-
    lection. 32mo 75
True Stories from New England History. 16mo,
    boards 45
Little Daffydowndilly, etc. 16mo, paper 15

Mrs. S. J. Higginson.
A Princess of Java. 12mo 1.50

Oliver Wendell Holmes.
Elsie Venner. A Romance of Destiny. Crown 8vo . 2.00
The Guardian Angel. Crown 8vo 2.00
The Story of Iris. 32mo 75
My Hunt after the Captain. 32mo 40
A Mortal Antipathy. Crown 8vo 1.50

Augustus Hoppin.
Recollections of Auton House. Illustrated. Small
    4to 1.25
A Fashionable Sufferer. Illustrated. 12mo . . . 1.50
Two Compton Boys. Illustrated. Small 4to . . . 1.50

Blanche Willis Howard.
One Summer. A Novel. New *Popular Edition.* Il-
    lustrated by Hoppin. 12mo 1.25

William Dean Howells.
Their Wedding Journey. Illustrated. 12mo . . . 1.50
The Same. "Little Classic" style. 18mo 1.00
A Chance Acquaintance. Illustrated. 12mo . . . 1.50
The Same. "Little Classic" style. 18mo 1.00
A Foregone Conclusion. 12mo 1.50
The Lady of the Aroostook. 12mo 1.50
The Undiscovered Country. 12mo 1.50
Suburban Sketches. 12mo 1.50
A Day's Pleasure, etc. 32mo 75

Thomas Hughes.
Tom Brown's School-Days at Rugby. Illustrated. 1.00
Tom Brown at Oxford. 16mo 1.25

Henry James, Jr.

A Passionate Pilgrim, and Other Tales. 12mo . .	$2.00
Roderick Hudson. 12mo	2.00
The American. 12mo	2.00
Watch and Ward. "Little Classic" style. 18mo .	1.25
The Europeans. 12mo	1.50
Confidence. 12mo	1.50
The Portrait of a Lady. 12mo	2.00

Anna Jameson.

Studies and Stories. New Edition. 16mo, gilt top .	1.25
Diary of an Ennuyée. New Edition. 16mo, gilt top .	1.25

Douglas Jerrold.

Mrs. Caudle's Curtain Lectures. Illustrated. 16mo .	1.00

Sarah Orne Jewett.

Deephaven. 18mo	1.25
Old Friends and New. 18mo	1.25
Country By-Ways. 18mo	1.25
The Mate of the Daylight. 18mo	1.25
A Country Doctor. 16mo	1.25
A Marsh Island. 16mo	1.25
A White Heron, and Other Stories. 18mo	1.25
The King of Folly Island, and Other People. 16mo	1.25

Rossiter Johnson.

"Little Classics."   Each in one volume.   18mo.

I. Exile.	X. Childhood.
II. Intellect.	XI. Heroism.
III. Tragedy.	XII. Fortune.
IV. Life.	XIII. Narrative Poems.
V. Laughter.	XIV. Lyrical Poems.
VI. Love.	XV. Minor Poems.
VII. Romance.	XVI. Nature.
VIII. Mystery.	XVII. Humanity.
IX. Comedy.	XVIII. Authors.

Each volume	1.00
The set	18.00

Joseph Kirkland.

Zury : the Meanest Man in Spring County. 12mo .	1.50
The McVeys. 16mo	1.25

Charles and Mary Lamb.

Tales from Shakespeare. 18mo	1.00
The Same. Illustrated. 16mo	1.00

Harriet and Sophia Lee.

Canterbury Tales. In three volumes. The set, 16mo $3.75

Henry Wadsworth Longfellow.

Hyperion. A Romance. 16mo 1.50
Popular Edition. 16mo 40
Popular Edition. Paper covers, 16mo 15
Outre-Mer. 16mo 1.50
Popular Edition. 16mo 40
Popular Edition. Paper covers, 16mo 15
Kavanagh. 16mo 1.50
Hyperion, Outre-Mer and Kavanagh. 2 vols. crown 8vo 3.00

Flora Haines Loughead.

The Man who was Guilty. 16mo 1.25

D. R. McAnally.

Irish Wonders. Illustrated. Small 4to 2.00

S. Weir Mitchell.

In War Time. 16mo 1.25
Roland Blake. 16mo 1.25

Lucy Gibbons Morse.

The Chezzles. Illustrated. . . . .

The Notable Series.

One Summer. By Blanche Willis Howard.
The Luck of Roaring Camp. By Bret Harte.
Backlog Studies. By C. D. Warner.
The set, 3 vols. 16mo 3.75

Mrs. M. O. W. Oliphant and T. B. Aldrich.

The Second Son. Crown 8vo 1.50

Elizabeth Stuart Phelps.

The Gates Ajar. 16mo 1.50
Beyond the Gates. 16mo 1.25
The Gates Between. 16mo 1.25
Men, Women, and Ghosts. 16mo 1.50
Hedged In. 16mo 1.50
The Silent Partner. 16mo 1.50
The Story of Avis. 16mo 1.50
Sealed Orders, and Other Stories. 16mo 1.50
Friends : A Duet. 16mo 1.25
Doctor Zay. 16mo 1.25
An Old Maid's Paradise, and Burglars in Paradise . 1.25
Madonna of the Tubs. Illustrated. 12mo 1.50
Jack the Fisherman. Illustrated. Square 12mo . . .50

Marian C. L. Reeves and Emily Read.

Pilot Fortune. 16mo $1.25

J. P. Quincy.

The Peckster Professorship. 16mo 1.25

Josiah Royce.

The Feud of Oakfield Creek. 16mo 1.25

Joseph Xavier Boniface Saintine.

Picciola. Illustrated. 16mo 1.00

Jacques Henri Bernardin de Saint-Pierre.

Paul and Virginia. Illustrated. 16mo 1.00
The Same, together with Undine, and Sintram. 32mo .75

Sir Walter Scott.

The Waverley Novels. *Illustrated Library Edition.*
Illustrated with 100 engravings by Darley, Dielman,
Fredericks, Low, Share, Sheppard. With glossary
and a full index of characters. In 25 volumes, 12mo.

Waverley.	The Antiquary.
Guy Mannering.	Rob Roy.
Old Mortality.	St. Ronan's Well.
Black Dwarf, and Legend	Redgauntlet.
of Montrose.	The Betrothed, and The
Heart of Mid-Lothian.	Highland Widow.
Bride of Lammermoor.	The Talisman, and Other
Ivanhoe.	Tales.
The Monastery.	Woodstock.
The Abbot.	The Fair Maid of Perth.
Kenilworth.	Anne of Geierstein.
The Pirate.	Count Robert of Paris.
The Fortunes of Nigel.	The Surgeon's Daughter,
Peveril of the Peak.	and Castle Dangerous.
Quentin Durward.	

Each volume 1.00
The set 25.00
Tales of a Grandfather. *Illustrated Library Edition.*
With six steel plates. In three volumes, 12mo . . 4.50

Horace E. Scudder.

The Dwellers in Five-Sisters' Court. 16mo 1.25
Stories and Romances. 16mo 1.25
The Children's Book. Edited by Mr. Scudder. Small
4to 2.50

Mark Sibley Severance.

Hammersmith: His Harvard Days. 12mo 1.50

J. E. Smith.
Oakridge : An Old-Time Story of Maine. 12mo . . $2.00

Mary A. Sprague.
An Earnest Trifler. 16mo 1.25

William W. Story.
Fiammetta. 16mo 1.25

Harriet Beecher Stowe.
Agnes of Sorrento. 12mo 1.50
The Pearl of Orr's Island. 12mo 1.50
Uncle Tom's Cabin. *Illustrated Edition.* 12mo . . 2.00
The Minister's Wooing. 12mo 1.50
The Mayflower, and Other Sketches. 12mo . . . 1.50
Dred. New Edition, from new plates. 12mo . . . 1.50
Oldtown Folks. 12mo 1.50
Sam Lawson's Fireside Stories. 12mo 1.50
My Wife and I. Illustrated. 12mo 1.50
We and Our Neighbors. Illustrated. 12mo . . . 1.50
Poganuc People. Illustrated. 12mo 1.50
The above eleven volumes, in box 16.00
Uncle Tom's Cabin. *Holiday Edition.* With Intro-
duction, and Bibliography by George Bullen, of the
British Museum. Over 100 Illustrations. 12mo . 3.00
The Same. *Popular Edition.* 12mo 1.00

Octave Thanet.
Knitters in the Sun. 16mo 1.25

Gen. Lew Wallace.
The Fair God ; or, The Last of the 'Tzins. 12mo . 1.50

Henry Watterson.
Oddities in Southern Life. Illustrated. 16mo . . . 1.50

Richard Grant White.
The Fate of Mansfield Humphreys, with the Episode
of Mr. Washington Adams in England. 16mo . . 1.25

Adeline D. T. Whitney.
Faith Gartney's Girlhood. Illustrated. 12mo . . . 1.50
Hitherto : A Story of Yesterdays. 12mo 1.50
Patience Strong's Outings. 12mo 1.50
The Gayworthys. 12mo 1.50
Leslie Goldthwaite. Illustrated. 12mo 1.50
We Girls : A Home Story. Illustrated. 12mo . . 1.50
Real Folks. Illustrated. 12mo 1.50

The Other Girls. Illustrated. 12mo $1.50
Sights and Insights. 2 vols. 12mo 3.00
Odd, or Even? 12mo 1.50
Boys at Chequasset. Illustrated. 12mo 1.50
Bonnyborough. 12mo 1.50
Homespun Yarns. Short Stories. 12mo 1.50

Justin Winsor.

Was Shakespeare Shapleigh? A Correspondence in
　Two Entanglements. Edited by Justin Winsor.
　Parchment-paper, 16mo 75

Lillie Chace Wyman.

Poverty Grass. 16mo 1.25

www.ingramcontent.com/pod-product-compliance
Lightning Source LLC
Chambersburg PA
CBHW031058280326
41928CB00049B/1108